THE SOAP OPERA digest SCRAPBOOK

John Kelly Genovese
and the Editors of Soap Opera Digest

Contemporary Books, Inc.
Chicago

Library of Congress Cataloging in Publication Data

Genovese, John Kelly.
   The Soap opera digest scrapbook.

   Includes Index.
   1. Soap operas--United States--Miscellanea.
I. Soap opera digest.   II. Title.
PN1992.8.S4G4   1984   791.45'5'05   84-17518
ISBN 0-8092-5385-2

The family trees were created prior to the printing of this publication; therefore there have been some changes in the relationships of the characters.

Family trees created by Andrea Wagner
Soap search puzzles created by Howard Wagner

Copyright © 1984 by Soap Opera Digest
All rights reserved
Published by Contemporary Books, Inc.
180 North Michigan Avenue, Chicago, Illinois 60601
Manufactured in the United States of America
Library of Congress Catalog Card Number: 84-17518
International Standard Book Number: 0-8092-5385-2

Published simultaneously in Canada by Beaverbooks, Ltd.
195 Allstate Parkway, Valleywood Business Park
Markham, Ontario L3R 4T8 Canada

CONTENTS

INTRODUCTION	viii
1. ALL MY CHILDREN	
Twenty Questions	1
Word Search	7
Family Tree	8
Soaptrivia #1: FROM WHENCE THEY CAME, PART I	10
2. ANOTHER WORLD	
Twenty Questions	13
Word Search	19
Family Tree	20
Photoquiz #1: BETTER HALVES	22
Soaptrivia #2: HELL HATH NO FURY. . . .	26
3. AS THE WORLD TURNS	
Twenty Questions	31
Crossword Puzzle	40
Family Tree	42
Soaptrivia #3: FILL IN THE BLANKS	44

4. CAPITOL
    Twenty Questions — 47
    Word Search — 53
    Family Tree — 54

Soaptrivia #4: WHAT A WAY TO GO — 56

5. DAYS OF OUR LIVES
    Twenty Questions — 59
    Crossword Puzzle — 64
    Family Tree — 66

Photoquiz #2: FAR FROM THE TREE — 68

Soaptrivia #5: THEY HAD TO START SOMEWHERE — 73

6. EDGE OF NIGHT
    Twenty Questions — 75
    Word Search — 81
    Family Tree — 82

Soaptrivia #6: THE OFFICIAL ROGUES' GALLERY OF MONTICELLO — 84

7. GENERAL HOSPITAL
    Twenty Questions — 87
    Crossword Puzzle — 92
    Family Tree — 94

Soaptrivia #7: HOW SOON WE FORGET — 96

8. GUIDING LIGHT
    Twenty Questions — 101
    Crossword Puzzle — 106
    Family Tree — 108

Soaptrivia #8: WHERE'S HOME? — 111

9. LOVING
    Twenty Questions — 113

Word Search	119
Family Tree	120

Soaptrivia #9: MISCELLANEOUS TRIVIA   122

10. ONE LIFE TO LIVE
Twenty Questions	125
Crossword Puzzle	130
Family Tree	132

Photoquiz #3: MOM ALWAYS LIKED YOU BEST   134

Soaptrivia #10: TRUE OR FALSE?   138

11. RYAN'S HOPE
Twenty Questions	141
Word Search	147
Family Tree	148

Photoquiz #4: THANKS FOR THE MEMORY   150

Soaptrivia #11: FROM WHENCE THEY CAME, PART II   152

12. SEARCH FOR TOMORROW
Twenty Questions	155
Word Search	161
Family Tree	162

Soaptrivia #12: MOUSTACHE TWIRLERS   164

13. THE YOUNG AND THE RESTLESS
Twenty Questions	169
Word Search	175
Family Tree	176

Photoquiz #5: FUN WHILE IT LASTED   178

ANSWERS   183

INDEX   203

INTRODUCTION

There are all sorts of soap opera viewers. There are those who randomly follow a few when they are home from work or school; those who have watched certain shows faithfully for many years; and those who switch channels between two, even three networks to see what's going on in all parts of the serial globe.

The Soap Opera Digest Scrapbook is dedicated to soap viewers of all ilks. It is our hope that wherever you, the reader, fit into the viewership scheme, you are able to relive great moments and recall timeless characters from your favorite soap. It is also our hope that you derive pleasure from picking up new points of information through our quizzes, which contain little-known historical facts that should add to your present enjoyment of this very vital broadcast medium.

Although many of our forthcoming questions are of a technical nature, concerning details of individual episodes, storylines, and character relationships, others are rooted in the wonderful little touches that add to the definition of the characters—their pastimes, their favorite drinks, their idiosyncrasies. Granted, a soap is nothing without story (good *or* bad), but the most winning element in the serial form is undoubtedly the time allotted for building characters and relationships.

INTRODUCTION

Without those ingredients, plot is nothing more than a shallow, haphazard excuse to shove svelte bodies in front of the cameras.

We at *Soap Opera Digest* believe that this book—replete with all the excitement, humor, and pathos of the medium it represents—reflects this philosophy. And as you go through this volume, picking up juicy "cocktail tidbits" about your favorite show, we think you're going to have one heck of a good time.

Ruth Warrick (Phoebe Wallingford)

1
ALL MY CHILDREN

Twenty Questions

1. Who informed Philip Brent of his true parentage?

    a. Phoebe Tyler
    b. Ruth Martin
    c. Nick Davis
    d. Erica Kane

2. Which of these characters married his late wife's twin sister?

    a. Lincoln Tyler
    b. Paul Martin
    c. Joe Martin
    d. Palmer Cortlandt

3. During Jeff and Erica's brief marriage, who were their down-to-earth neighbors?

    a. Lou and Sam Beck
    b. Ruth and Ted Brent
    c. Harriet and Al McFadden
    d. Edie and Bill Hoffman

THE **SOAP OPERA** *Digest* SCRAPBOOK

4. *What was the name of Kate Martin's deceased husband?*

    a. Harry   c. Eddie
    b. Henry   d. Skip

5. *Who was the only character who addressed Charles Tyler as "Charlie"?*

    a. Kate Martin   c. Phoebe Tyler
    b. Mona Tyler   d. Joe Martin

6. *What disease afflicted Chuck seriously enough for Tara to remain married to him despite her love for Philip?*

    a. alcoholism   c. kidney disease
    b. schizophrenia   d. dysentery

7. *What was the main cause of Nick and Anne's divorce?*

    a. his preoccupation with his son, Philip
    b. her lingering feelings for Paul
    c. her obsession with having a child
    d. his long hours at the Chateau

8. *Where did Eric Kane, Erica's errant father, reside before his death?*

    a. Center City   c. Europe
    b. New York City   d. New Orleans

9. *Who was the white man who married Nancy Grant, a black divorcée, on his deathbed?*

    a. Jim Ousley   c. Russ Anderson
    b. David Thornton   d. Carl Blair

ALL MY CHILDREN

Now You See Them, Now You Don't

Soapland is notorious for characters who disappear into thin air and are never mentioned again, but two particular cases really take the honors. In the first year of *All My Children* Dr. Joe Martin (Ray MacDonnell) had a young son, Bobby, who was never seen. He was always alleged to be upstairs doing his homework. After a while the powers-that-be decided that Bobby was not necessary to the plot, and he was never mentioned again. Also, during the first month of *Capitol* the four McCandless brothers had a younger adopted sister, Gillian (Kelly Palzis), who soon went the way of Bobby Martin. We can only assume she's up in the attic, helping poor Bobby with the algebra problem he's been working on since 1970!

10. Which one of these men was never one of Erica's "conquests"?

    a. Philip Brent   c. Brandon Kingsley
    b. Tom Cudahy   d. Wally McFadden

11. Which one of these young women, as a little girl, inadvertently thwarted her father's plan to poison her mother?

    a. Dottie Thornton   c. Carrie Sanders
    b. Jenny Gardner   d. Liza Colby

12. What is the name of Phoebe's unseen society friend?

    a. Juanita Redway   c. Colleen Ramsey
    b. Juanita Ramsey   d. Pauline Rysdale

13. Which one of these men never physically abused a woman?

    a. Ray Gardner   c. Gil Barrett
    b. Billy Clyde Tuggle   d. Adrian Shepherd

14. How did Ruth and Joe Martin meet their adopted son, Tad?

    a. He was left on their doorstep by his father, Ray Gardner.
    b. He was Joe's patient after having been beaten up by Billy Clyde Tuggle.
    c. He was an unwanted child originally cared for by Jeff Martin and his second wife, Mary.
    d. Ruth found him wandering around a supermarket in an amnesia-induced daze.

15. Which former flame of Cliff Warner's did Palmer Cortlandt bribe to claim she had had Cliff's child?

    a. Sybil Thorne   c. Devon McFadden
    b. Janice Rawlins   d. Betsy Kennicott

16. Which misfortune has not befallen Brooke Cudahy?

    a. She discovered her mother was a drug mobster who was out to kill her.
    b. She was abducted by a fiend obsessed with her.
    c. She was attacked by her husband's sexually warped pal.
    d. She fell for a man who turned out to be her brother.

17. Which enterprise does not exist in Pine Valley?

    a. Gibson's restaurant
    b. The Serving Spoon gourmet shop and cafe
    c. The Goal Post restaurant
    d. The Boutique

ALL MY CHILDREN

Julia Barr (Brooke Cudahy)

18. What is the name of Edna Ferguson's rich Southern ex?

    a. Hank   c. Pete
    b. Frank   d. Benny

19. What is the name of the sleazy Center City bar frequented by a few Pine Valley residents, and who is the bartender?

    a. Foxy's; Bud
    b. Foxy's; Hughie
    c. The Pink Flamingo; Freddie
    d. Harry's; Pete

20. Which one of these women was never a hooker?

    a. Donna Tyler   c. Lettie Jean
    b. Estelle Sago   d. Myrtle Fargate

Agnes Nixon's *All My Children* has been consistently popular because of its generation-based stories, which vary tremendously in content and age appeal.

Palmer Cortlandt (James Mitchell, above), Pine Valley's wealthy but rarely mirth-bearing Santa Claus, fought bitterly to shatter the marriage of his daughter and son-in-law, Nina and Cliff Warner (Taylor Miller and Peter Bergman, at right).

Ellen Dalton (Kathleen Noone, below, at left) is usually supportive of her daughter, Devon, a reformed alcoholic. But Dottie Thornton (Tasia Valenza) isn't so lucky—her mother once went so far as to pay a young stud to squire Dottie around town!

Photo by Andrea Wagner

Photo by Leslie Murray

ALL MY CHILDREN

All My Children Word Search

Soap-related words are hidden in this maze of letters. They read forward, backward, up, down, or diagonally, always in a straight line. Circle the letters as you find them. Letters may be used more than once. The remaining letters will (in order) spell a hidden message. To start, we have indicated the first word in bold type. Enjoy!

```
T D N A L T R O C R E M L A P
W S C E R E N R A W A N I N E
S N O S L E N G E R G L C E I
Y T C P C N A I L L I G L D G
H O A M L S E K U D E L C D N
A T I R I A O L R O E H S A A
D R N P F I O E N N A T E F E
U E E C F V T G D N E V Y C N
C L S H E N S A D A K N C M A
E Y S U E R L L M P N S H N K
K T E C E T E P S E I Y A O A
O A J K O R I A J S G X T V C
O N N N S T M A L C H O E E I
R O L E C A S I N O T F A D R
B M Y K C I R R A W H T U R E
```

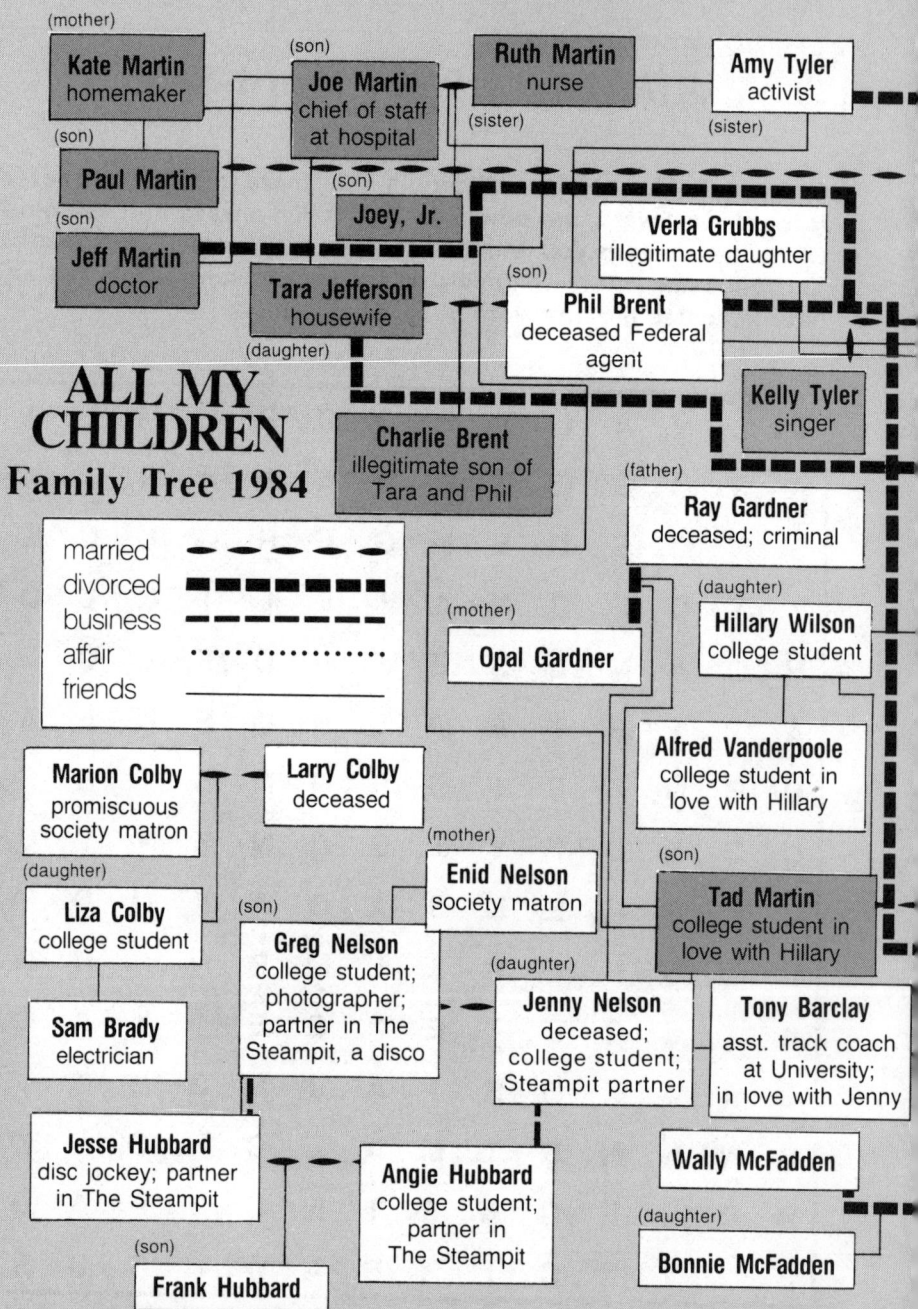

ALL MY CHILDREN

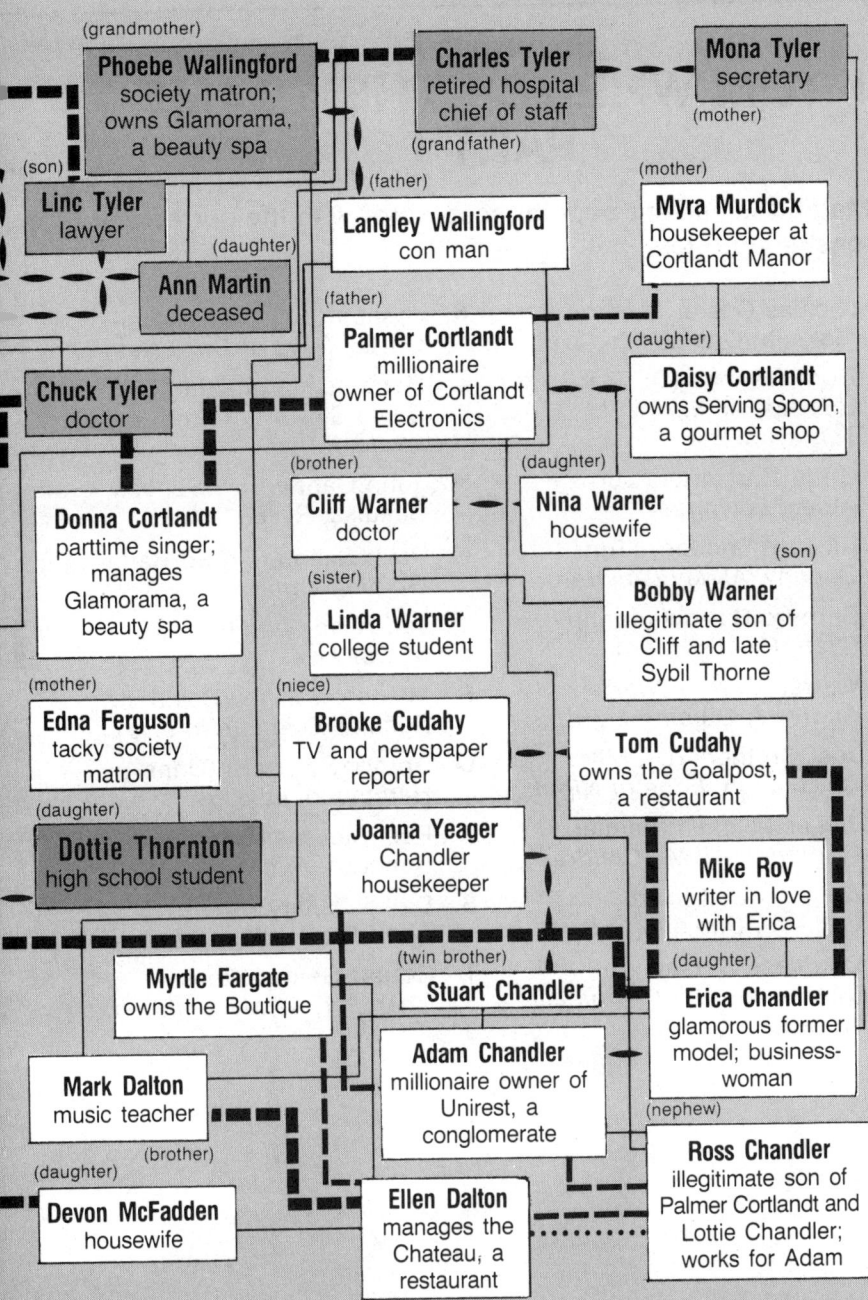

THE SOAP OPERA *Digest* SCRAPBOOK

Soaptrivia #1
FROM WHENCE THEY CAME, PART I

Match the current popular soap actor with the correct list of past soap roles.

- **A.** Nicolas Coster (Anthony Makana, *One Life to Live*)
- **B.** Don Hastings (Dr. Bob Hughes, *As the World Turns*)
- **C.** Chris Marcantel (Curtis Alden, *Loving*)
- **D.** Richard Shoberg (Tom Cudahy, *All My Children*)
- **E.** Bernard Barrow (Johnny Ryan, *Ryan's Hope*)
- **F.** Warren Burton (Warren Andrews, *Guiding Light*)
- **G.** Joel Crothers (Dr. Miles Cavanaugh, *Edge of Night*)
- **H.** James Mitchell (Palmer Cortlandt, *All My Children*)
- **I.** Anthony Call (Herb Callison, *One Life to Live*)
- **J.** Douglass Watson (Mackenzie Cory, *Another World*)
- **K.** Joseph Gallison (Dr. Neil Curtis, *Days of Our Lives*)
- **L.** Henderson Forsythe (Dr. David Stewart, *As the World Turns*)
- **M.** John Gabriel (Dr. Seneca Beaulac, *Ryan's Hope*)
- **N.** Peter Simon (Dr. Ed Bauer, *Guiding Light*)
- **O.** Jed Allan (Don Craig, *Days of Our Lives*)
- **P.** Michael Zaslow (David Renaldi, *One Life to Live*)
- **Q.** Anthony Herrera (Dane Hammond, *Loving*)
- **R.** Paul Stevens (Brian Bancroft, *Another World*)
- **S.** David Canary (Adam Chandler, *All My Children*)
- **T.** Robert Gentry (Ross Chandler, *All My Children*)

SOAPTRIVIA

1. Colin Whitney, *Edge of Night*; Dr. Joe Werner, *Guiding Light*
2. Far Wind, *The Doctors*; Steven Frame, *Another World*
3. Jack Lane, *Edge of Night*
4. Scott Phillips, *Search for Tomorrow*; Ian McFarland, *As the World Turns*
5. Bill Matthews, *Another World*; Tom Edwards, *One Life to Live*; Steven Cord, *Return to Peyton Place*
6. Dr. Matt Steele, *Young Doctor Malone*; Paul Britton, *The Secret Storm*; John Eldredge, *Our Private World*; Robert Delaney, *Another World*; Robert Delaney, *Somerset*
7. Tim Brannigan, *The Secret Storm*; Mark Galloway, *As the World Turns*; Jack Curtis, *The Young and the Restless*; James Stenbeck, *As the World Turns*
8. Tim Werner, *Guiding Light*; Pete Shea, *Another World*
9. Martin Spode, *Edge of Night*; Jim Benson, *From These Roots*
10. Brad Murphy, *The Doctors*; Dr. Ed Bauer, *Guiding Light*; Dr. John Carr, *A World Apart*; Philip Lyons, *Another World*
11. Mitch Farmer, *Somerset*; Kevin Jamison, *Edge of Night*
12. Link Morrison, *Love of Life*; Teddy Holmes, *General Hospital*
13. Dick Hart, *Search for Tomorrow*; Dr. Pete Chernak, *Love Is a Many Splendored Thing*; Roger Thorpe, *Guiding Light*
14. Dan Kincaid, *The Secret Storm*; Ira Paulson, *Edge of Night*
15. Steve Hurley, *Love Is a Many Splendored Thing*; Dr. Bruce Henderson, *The Young and the Restless*
16. Dr. Robert Wallace, *Moment of Truth*; Walter Haskins, *Search for Tomorrow*; Dr. John Carpenter, *Edge of Night*
17. Ace Hubbard, *Love of Life*; Paul Britton, *The Secret Storm*
18. Joe Haskell, *Dark Shadows*; Ken Stevens, *The Secret Storm*; Julian Cannell, *Somerset*
19. Lloyd Griffin, *Edge of Night*; Julian Hathaway, *Where the Heart Is*
20. Eddie Dorrance, *All My Children*; Jason Dunlap, *Another World*

Irene Dailey (Liz Matthews) and Douglass Watson (Mac Cory)

2
ANOTHER WORLD

Twenty Questions

1. *Pat Matthews met her longtime husband, John Randolph, when he defended her for killing a man in a fit of temporary insanity. Who was the man, and what was the motive?*

    a. Ken Baxter; he performed a butcher abortion on Pat, which left her sterile.

    b. Tom Baxter; he fathered her child and convinced her to have a butcher abortion, which left her sterile.

    c. Tim Baxter; he fathered another woman's child.

    d. Howard Baxter; he fathered another woman's child.

2. *When Danny Fargo played his con games with his confused wife, Missy, what did he do for her in lieu of writing IOU's?*

    a. He bought her a pizza.

    b. He took her to B-movies at an old theater.

    c. He had sex with her.

    d. He wrote her a corny song.

THE SOAP OPERA *Digest* SCRAPBOOK

3. *Whom did Liz Matthews hope her son, Bill, would marry instead of Missy?*

    a. Lenore Moore
    b. Lahoma Vane
    c. Lee Randolph
    d. Peggy Nolan

4. *What was Jim Matthews's line of work?*

    a. CPA
    b. corporate lawyer
    c. criminal lawyer
    d. labor relations mediator

5. *Sam Lucas, Ada's ex-con brother, worked at what menial job to put himself through law school?*

    a. garage mechanic at Ernie's
    b. construction worker for Frame Enterprises
    c. band boy for the house band at the Bay City Country Club
    d. busboy at the Top of the Tower restaurant

6. *Whom did Rachel marry after divorcing Russ Matthews?*

    a. Steven Frame
    b. Mackenzie Cory
    c. Walter Curtin
    d. Ted Clark

7. *This show, more than any other, has shared characters with other serials; it also has spun off two new shows:* Somerset *and* Texas. *Which of these characters never appeared on another show, even for a guest shot?*

    a. Robert Delaney

ANOTHER WORLD

"Not with a Bang but a Whimper"

After Steven Frame (George Reinholt) was killed off on *Another World*, headwriter Harding ("Pete") Lemay kept introducing more and more siblings for the deceased in order to keep the family alive. Then, a few years later, Frame turned up alive (in the person of actor David Canary) and a new headwriter regime was in power. Nobody called, or even mentioned, any of the other Frames who had, by then, departed Bay City. So much for an important story family.

    b.   Mackenzie Cory
    c.   Iris Carrington
    d.   Mitchell Dru

8. Bay City is a real setting, unlike many in serials. In what state is Bay City located?

    a. Michigan
    b. Ohio
    c. Illinois
    d. Indiana

9. Walter Curtin defended his wife, Lenore, for the murder of Wayne Addison. Who was Addison's killer?

    a. Lenore Curtin
    b. Walter Curtin
    c. Bernice Robinson
    d. Quincy Stoner

THE SOAP OPERA *Digest* SCRAPBOOK

10. *What evil plot did Caroline Johnson, Michael and Marianne Randolph's baby-sitter, hatch against her employers?*

    a. to murder the children in their beds as a sort of sick revenge for a tragedy in her own life, get Pat drunk, and frame Pat for the crime

    b. to murder Pat and John and become the children's legal guardian

    c. to make it appear that Pat and Sam Lucas were having an affair, so John would divorce Pat and marry Caroline

    d. to murder Pat so she could have John and the children

11. *Sally Frame, Alice's adopted daughter, is biologically the granddaughter of what former Bay City resident?*

    a. Helen Moore
    b. Beatrice Gordon
    c. Louise Goddard
    d. Sylvie Kosloff

12. *For what chronic disease did Alice treat Dennis Carrington during his childhood in New York?*

    a. asthma
    b. gout
    c. congenital heart disease
    d. anemia

13. *Which of these characters was never romantically involved with Jamie Frame?*

    a. Marianne Randolph
    b. Blaine Ewing
    c. Susan Shearer
    d. Gwen Parrish

14. *Who was Tic deCosgrove in relation to Iris?*

    a. her New York society friend
    b. her chauffeur
    c. the man she hired to bug Eliot Carrington's suite
    d. the gigolo she hired to seduce Rachel away from Mac

ANOTHER WORLD

15. Which of these well-meaning ladies was never portrayed as a buttinsky mother?

    a. Leueen Parrish
    b. Liz Matthews
    c. Elena dePoulignac
    d. Rose Perrini

16. Who were all the Frame offspring, and from what hick town did they hail?

    a. Emma, Steven, Sharlene, Vince, Willis, Janice; Chadwell
    b. Steven, Sharlene, Molly, Willis, Vince, Janice; Hadley
    c. Steven, Vince, Willis, Janice, Carol; Chadds Ford
    d. Emma, Steven, Molly, Vince, Willis; Atwell

17. Why did Rachel make love to Mitch Blake on that one night their son, Matthew, was conceived?

    a. She was convinced Mac would never leave Janice for her.
    b. She did it so that Mitch would help her save Mac from Janice's murderous scheme.
    c. She was forced to do so by Janice, who held them at gunpoint so she could take their picture and give it to Mac.
    d. She believed Mac was sterile; and she desperately wanted to give Amanda a brother or sister.

18. What were the two last names used by the Nazi art-smuggling family that threatened Louis St. George?

    a. Nordmann and Petersen
    b. Krebbs and Petersen
    c. Krebbs and Nordmann
    d. Richter and Nordmann

THE SOAP OPERA *Digest* SCRAPBOOK

Gretchen Oehler (Vivien Gorrow)

19. Which one of these men never married Ada?

    a. Ernie Downs
    b. Jim Matthews
    c. Gil McGowan
    d. Charlie Hobson

20. Which one of these men never partook of Felicia Gallant's sexual favors?

    a. Mackenzie Cory
    b. Gil Fenton
    c. Cass Winthrop
    d. Carl Hutchins

ANOTHER WORLD

Another World Word Search

Soap-related words are hidden in this maze of letters. They read forward, backward, up, down, or diagonally, always in a straight line. Circle the letters as you find them. Letters may be used more than once. The remaining letters will (in order) spell a hidden message. To start, we have indicated the first word in bold type. Enjoy!

B	S	W	H	N	C	O	N	A	D	**A**	D	N	I	L
A	I	Y	T	I	C	Y	A	B	**N**	I	G	G	I	W
N	N	N	A	V	A	N	R	**N**	T	R	R	F	B	L
C	G	D	E	E	U	O	**A**	E	M	O	R	L	I	U
R	L	H	D	K	O	**S**	S	A	B	A	A	A	S	A
O	E	A	E	K	**T**	N	H	E	M	I	G	T	G	P
F	T	M	L	**U**	I	G	R	E	N	L	R	N	U	L
T	O	Y	**A**	H	N	T	I	E	I	U	I	B	R	A
L	N	**R**	C	I	A	Z	E	A	S	L	L	E	D	N
O	**T**	T	B	F	N	W	M	T	T	I	V	L	O	E
E	U	Y	L	E	I	K	F	A	S	S	U	O	L	C
H	O	A	K	N	C	U	C	H	R	I	S	C	I	R
R	C	C	G	A	N	A	I	L	U	J	R	I	V	A
K	A	V	L	D	I	N	F	O	R	T	U	N	E	S
M	V	B	S	E	G	A	I	R	R	A	M	E	R	H

19

THE SOAP OPERA *Digest* SCRAPBOOK

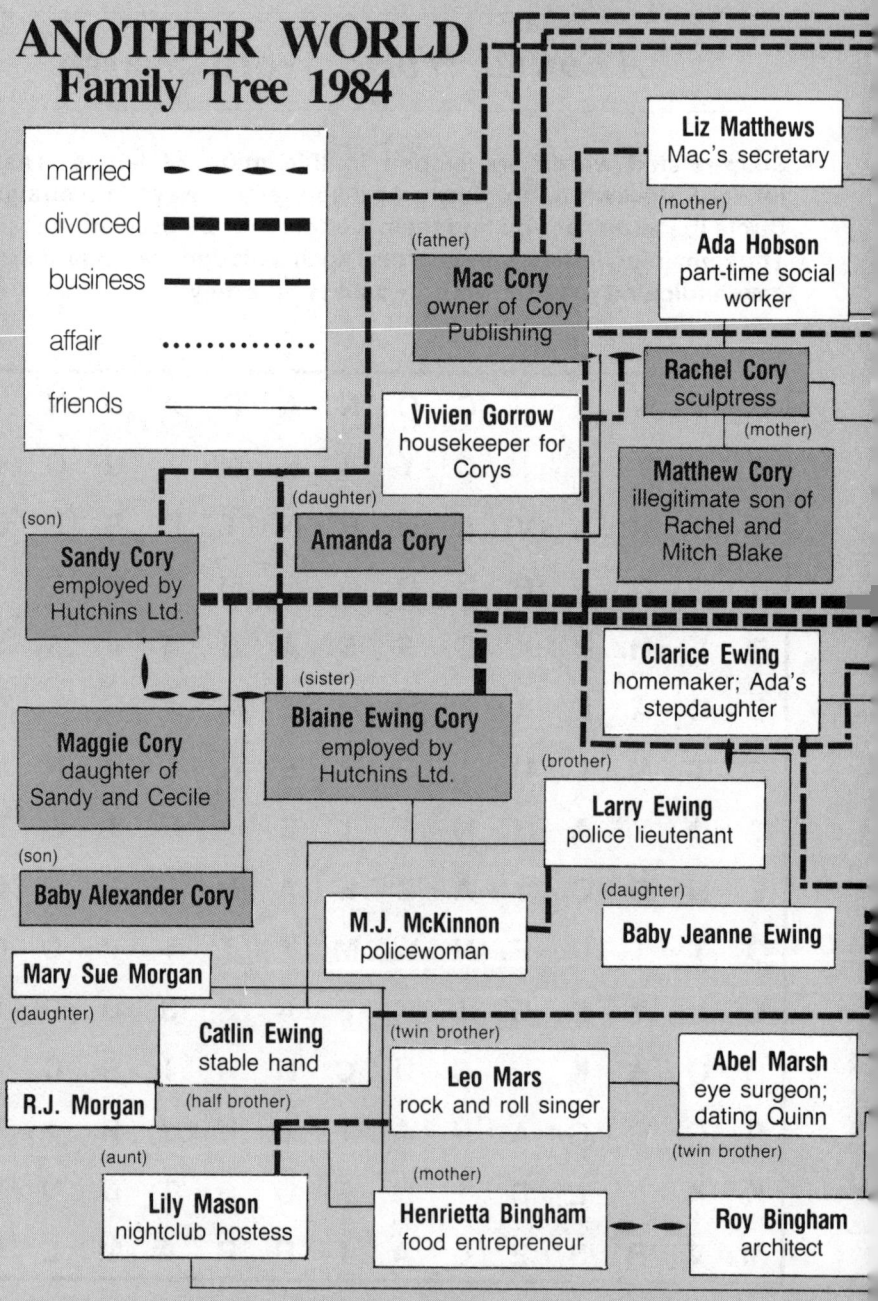

20

ANOTHER WORLD

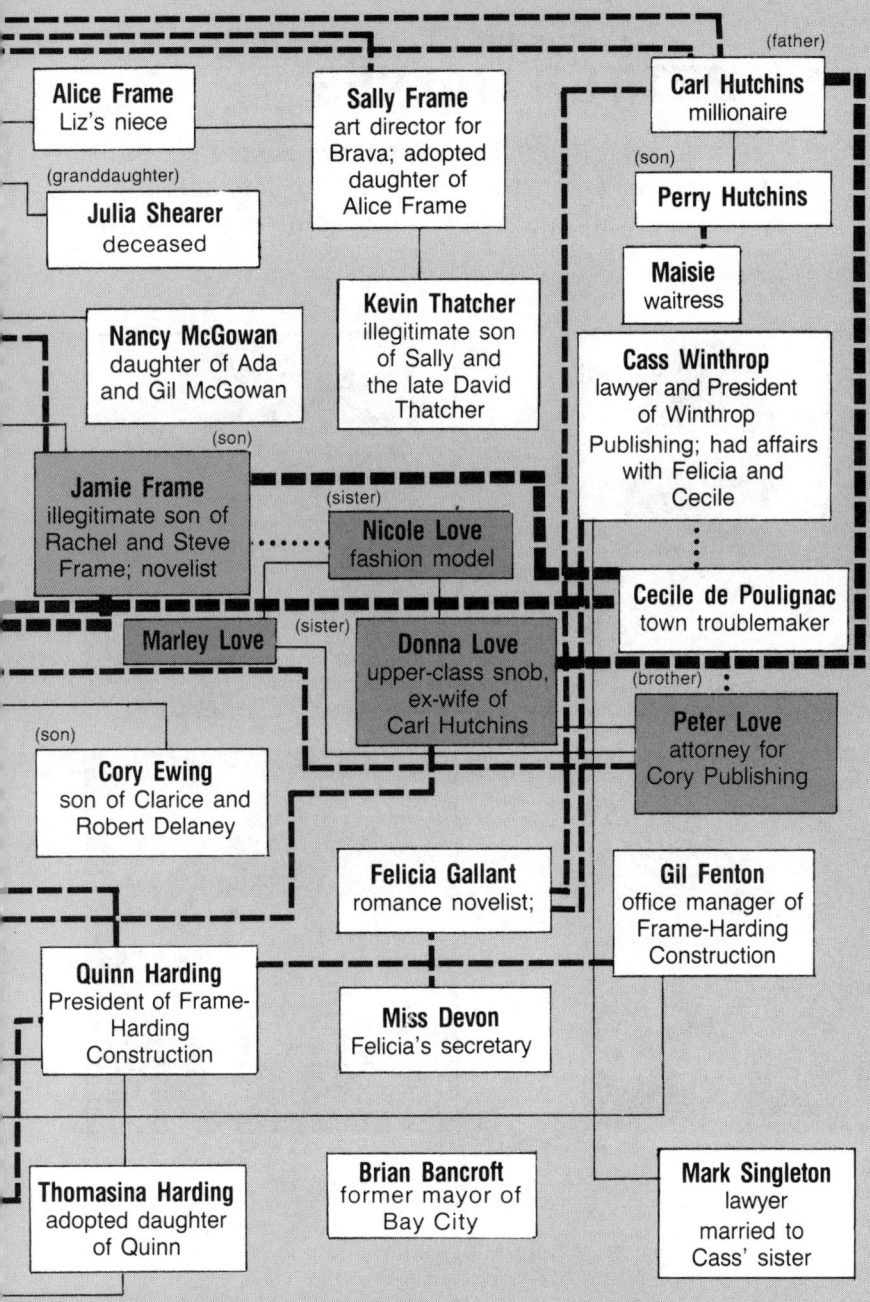

THE SOAP OPERA *Digest* SCRAPBOOK

Photoquiz #1
BETTER HALVES

Behind every successful man is a supportive woman, or so the assumption goes. Match the hubby in the left column with his respective distaff side in the right column.

A

1

B

Photo by Martha Swope

2

Photo by ABC Visual Communication

PHOTOQUIZ

THE **SOAP OPERA** *Digest* SCRAPBOOK

6

F

Photo by Kacey Associates Inc.

7

G

PHOTOQUIZ

H

8

Photo by Kacey Associates Inc.

I

Photo by Andrea Wagner

9

THE SOAP OPERA *Digest* SCRAPBOOK

Soaptrivia # 2
HELL HATH NO FURY....

Although many of these controversial females have since redeemed themselves for their past sins, none of them are as pure as the driven snow; they can turn mean again at any time. Match the infamous "bitch goddess" with her correct track record of evil.

A. Erica Kane, *All My Children*
B. Dorian Callison, *One Life to Live*
C. Rachel Cory, *Another World*
D. Dr. Monica Quartermaine, *General Hospital*
E. Jill Abbott, *The Young and the Restless*
F. Myrna Clegg, *Capitol*
G. Liz Matthews, *Another World*
H. Phoebe Wallingford, *All My Children*
I. Raven Whitney, *Edge of Night*
J. Karen Dixon, *As the World Turns*
K. Nola Chamberlain, *Guiding Light*
L. Stephanie Wyatt, *Search for Tomorrow*
M. Bobbie Spencer, *General Hospital*
N. Rae Woodard, *Ryan's Hope*
O. Cecile dePoulignac, *Another World*
P. Paula Denning, *Capitol*
Q. Liza Colby, *All My Children*
R. Lisa McColl, *As the World Turns*
S. Vanessa Lewis, *Guiding Light*
T. Donna Love, *Another World*

1. Looked down her nose at her prospective sister-in-law to the point of digging up dirt on her past; indulged her stepson against her ex-husband's wishes; hired a gold-digging schemer to seduce her brother away from his intended
2. Faked agoraphobia to perpetuate a loveless marriage; shot her husband's true love; killed her housekeeper
3. Purposely became pregnant by a man she didn't love in order to trap a man she really loved; feigned friendship toward the girlfriend of the man she tried to trap

4. Became the nagging wife of a hardworking intern; had a brief fling with a heel who had become a shoe tycoon; tried to turn her son against his father; briefly married a rich, mother-dominated Chicago lawyer; had an affair with an opportunistic married man whom she herself eventually married and for whose murder she was unjustly tried

5. Became the nagging wife of a hardworking intern; had a one-night stand with her husband's brother-in-law, which produced a son; ruined her second marriage because of greed and lust toward her child's father; disapproved so vehemently of her daughter-in-law that she hired the girl's sleazy ex-flame to shatter her son's marriage

6. Became the nagging wife of a hardworking intern; had a brief fling with her boss, for whose murder her husband was unjustly tried; had a nervous breakdown when her second husband couldn't shake the memory of his first true love; fell in love with a kind, sensitive man who turned out to be her brother; ruined her third marriage because she had a hot involvement with her married boss; two-timed her married lover with his professional rival, who ended up murdered

7. Jilted her fiancé for a rich man who saved her father's ailing business; resumed her affair with her ex-fiancé, whom she schemed to keep from the woman he truly cared about; had a fling with an ex-trucker whom she tried to keep under her thumb both professionally and romantically; tried to undermine a male business superior through proxy fights

8. Tried but failed to seduce her stepbrother; married a budding politico for his money and connections; became pregnant by someone even more ambitious and eventually married him; destroyed her marriage by having an affair with a gigolo, who ended up dead; tried to "sell" her baby to her stepbrother and his wife

9. Destroyed her lover's political career when he resumed an old relationship; left her illegitimate daughter in the care of her mother; took an ambitious young lover who also made whoopee with her daughter; tried to ruin a doctor's career when he realized skeletons in her closet were behind a young girl's deteriorated emotional condition

10. Lost her medical career when she and her medic lover covered up an error that cost a patient her life; became the mortal enemy of the doctor who had fallen in love with that

patient; married an older man for his money; left her husband to die of a stroke when he discovered she had concocted lies to turn him against his illegitimate son, whom he had ill-advisedly cut out of his will; tried to seduce, and in one case succeeded in seducing, two men who at various times were married to the stepdaughter she resented; used the vast power she had inherited from her late husband to harm professionally the people she wrongly blamed for her empty emotional life; manipulated her younger sister to such an extent that the girl frequently had to be institutionalized; tarnished an already stormy marriage by trying to win back the man who had fathered her daughter

11. Concocted lies about her romantic rival; falsely cried "attempted rape" toward the concerned friend of the young man she tried to snare; swore she would get revenge against her lover when she discovered he preferred her own mother as a bedmate

12. Hastily married her lover's brother when he was falsely presumed dead; pushed her lover's intended down a flight of stairs after the lover turned up alive; briefly took up again with her lover after he had married, thereby provoking her jealous husband to try to kill both her and the lover

13. Tried to win back a happily married old flame by falsely claiming he had fathered her daughter; threatened to stash her stepmother in an old folks' home when Stepmama discovered her scheme; brief gained almost half of a company's stocks through her brief marriage to the black sheep son of a deceased tycoon; married the brother-in-law of the widow whose husband this bitch had tried to slap with paternity; sold her company proxies to her materialistic lover, who accidentally shot her husband dead; unwittingly created a Frankenstein in her daughter, who was transformed from an innocent into a tantalizing homewrecker

14. Faked pregnancy by a young doctor; blackmailed a millionaire into marriage, only to have him lose his ill-gotten fortune; married the millionaire's nemesis

15. Seduced the rich husband of a lonely woman who had taken her under her wing; blamed the woman for causing the accident that killed the man; seduced and married her mother's male friend, whom she caused to have a heart attack; had an affair with a man with whom she conspired to

financially drain her deceased lover's widow, only to have him marry the widow; had an affair with a sly user, married his father for his money, then resumed her affair with his son

16. Faked pregnancy by a young lawyer; faked blindness to trap another lover into marriage
17. Married a man for his money; fed her husband's drug dependency while she had an affair with his brother; married the brother and had a child, then sued him unsuccessfully for custody; fell for a man she had planned to seduce only briefly
18. Conspired with her stepson to blackmail a politico who patronized hookers behind his wife's back; manipulated her archenemy's mentally unstable romantic rival; schemed to keep her daughter from marrying the archenemy's son; bribed her husband's ex-lover and illegitimate daughter to leave town
19. Purposely upset her "unsuitable" prospective daughter-in-law by digging up her long-lost mother; furnished the DA with damning evidence against the same girl, who was unjustly tried for the murder of her con-man husband; faked illness so this girl, now her daughter-in-law, could wait on her hand and foot; contributed to the breakup of her former male friend's marriage to her confused daughter; became briefly infatuated with her boss, who married her nephew's gold-digging ex
20. Purposely upset her "unsuitable" daughter-in-law by hiring a woman to pose as the girl's mother; nagged her husband to the point where he fell for his secretary; faked paralysis to keep her husband by her side; encouraged her niece to steal the husband of her romantic rival's daughter

Don Hastings (Dr. Bob Hughes)

3
AS THE WORLD TURNS

Twenty Questions

1. Which is true about *Nancy and Chris Hughes?*
    a. They have three children; Donald, Penny, and Bob.
    b. They had four children, but their other son John was fatally thrown from a horse at Pa Hughes's Illinois farm.
    c. They had four children, but their other daughter Susan drowned in a pool during an electrical storm.
    d. They had five children, but their twin boys, John and Bill, died in a fire at the family farm.

2. *Although Nancy dearly loved her father-in-law, what did Pa Hughes constantly do that irritated her?*
    a. washed his hands in her kitchen sink
    b. brought home stray mutts for her to feed
    c. played Sammy Kaye records full blast in his basement workshop
    d. gave Bob a dollar to slip him a shot of whiskey when Nancy wasn't looking

3. Which was not true of Judge Lowell, Ellen Stewart's wise grandfather?

   a. He brought Chris into his thriving law practice.
   b. He liked fine sherry.
   c. He read mystery novels.
   d. He prodded his weak son, Jim, to divorce Claire and marry Chris's sister, Edith.

4. Why did Jeff Baker leave his wife, Penny Hughes, and where did he go to escape from his problems?

   a. His dominating mother, Grace, lied to him that Penny was seeing Tom Pope behind his back; to an out-of-town bar, where he became the resident drunk.
   b. Grace had told Penny that Jeff was a flop in the family business; to a bar where he got a job playing piano.
   c. Grace had fired Jeff from the family business; to a farm where he fell for a fragile disabled girl.
   d. Grace blamed Jeff for the bankruptcy of the family business; to an out-of-town bar where he became a bartender.

5. Why did Donald resent Nancy for a long time?

   a. When he was younger she made him break off with Janice, an older woman; he later married her, but she quickly died.
   b. When he was younger she made him break off with Janice, a 16-year-old girl he loved; he later planned to marry her, but she died on the eve of the wedding.
   c. When he was younger she annulled his marriage to Janice, an older woman; when he located her years later she was on her deathbed.
   d. She had encouraged Janice, an older woman, to lead him

AS THE WORLD TURNS

> ## Another Flub
>
> In the early '70s, *As the World Turns* featured a handsome, romantic lead who played a sympathetic doctor. Unfortunately, a fight scene with a patient's disgruntled husband sent our hero's toupé flying on live TV. The bald thespian disappeared from soapland, the "rug" pulled out from under him.

on and dump him just to teach him a lesson about his inflated male ego.

6. *Where was Lisa's hometown?*

    a. Centerville

    b. Flat Rock

    c. Louisville, Kentucky

    d. Rockford, Illinois

7. *What are the correct circumstances of Dan Stewart's parentage?*

    a. Ellen and David conceived Dan during David's marriage to his first wife, Betty.

    b. Ellen and Tim Cole conceived Dan out of wedlock, and he was adopted by David and Betty Stewart; later Ellen and Tim married and tried to get Dan back but failed; in time Tim and Betty died; and Ellen married David.

    c. David and Betty conceived Dan out of wedlock; Betty died, and David married Ellen.

    d. Tim Cole and his first wife, Louise, conceived Dan, but Louise died in childbirth; Tim married Ellen and died; Ellen married David, and they raised Dan as theirs.

THE SOAP OPERA *Digest* SCRAPBOOK

Henderson Forsythe (Dr. David Stewart)

8. Who was Bob's first patient?

   a. Alma Miller
   b. Claire Cassen
   c. Judge Lowell
   d. Rose Brando

9. Why did Dr. Doug Cassen favor Neil Wade over Bob as a protégé?

   a. Neil had saved Judge Lowell's life.
   b. Bob became too emotionally involved with his patients.
   c. Doug believed Neil had had to struggle harder than Bob to get where he was.
   d. Neil was secretly Doug's illegitimate son.

AS THE WORLD TURNS

10. *Who told Dan the truth about his origins?*

    a. Michael Shea

    b. John Dixon

    c. David Stewart

    d. Franny Brennan

11. *With what song did Claire identify during the lonely period after Doug's death?*

    a. "Drinking Again"

    b. "People"

    c. "Lost in the Stars"

    d. "It's All Over Now"

Without Parole

In the early '80s *As the World Turns* had a convoluted plot involving an insidious cocaine ring at Memorial Hospital. It involved a multitude of characters, including Dr. Larry Travis (Gary Lahti), who was in prison for a drug crime for which he had been framed by Dr. Rick Ryan (Gary Hudson). Succeeding headwriters who inherited the storyline, however, were so confounded by it that they continued only a few threads while letting others fall by the wayside. As a result, both characters faded away. For all we know, Travis is still rotting in the slammer!

THE SOAP OPERA Digest SCRAPBOOK

Ellen Stewart (Patricia Bruder) may be a model mother and grandmother on *As the World Turns,* but her past reads like a novel. Once she fatally bopped a blackmailing romantic rival over the head with a vase when the victim threatened to tell Dan Stewart he was Ellen's illegitimate son!

12. *Which is not true of Tom Hughes?*

    a. He went through a hippie stage.

    b. He voluntarily joined the army.

    c. He lived with an older woman in New York until Lisa put a stop to the arrangement.

    d. He practiced law in Europe for a while.

13. *Who was the father of Barbara Stenbeck, Bob's stepdaughter?*

    a. Rick Ryan, Bob's professional nemesis

    b. Chuck Ryan, Bob's deceased buddy from medical school

    c. Michael Shea, Bob's professional nemesis

    d. Dick Martin, Donald's professional and romantic rival

AS THE WORLD TURNS

14. *Which is not an Oakdale restaurant?*

    a. The Plaka
    b. The Rodeo
    c. The Colonnade Room
    d. Armando's

15. *Which is* not *true of the dichotomous John Dixon?*

    a. He kidnapped Andrew, his and Kim's son, from Kim before her marriage to Dan Stewart.
    b. He provided false evidence against Bob in a malpractice suit.
    c. He discovered that James Stenbeck was Greta Aldrin's son and that Gunnar Stenbeck was the rightful Stenbeck heir.
    d. He blackmailed Natalie Bannon, during her marriage to Tom Hughes, with his knowledge that her first husband, Ralph Porter, had committed suicide because she had had an affair with his married brother, Luke.

16. *What did Nancy do every time she was perplexed by a family problem?*

    a. She worked out her frustrations by pounding dough for a fresh coffee cake.
    b. She confided her worries to Alma as they sipped sherry in Alma's living room.
    c. She helped Pa Hughes in his workshop.
    d. She called her sister Pearl in Kansas City.

THE SOAP OPERA *Digest* SCRAPBOOK

17. Why did Joyce shoot Donald during their disastrous marriage?

    a. She mistook him for an intruder.

    b. She mistook him for Ralph Mitchell, her ex-lover, who planned to tell Donald of their affair.

    c. She was devastated that Donald wanted to leave her for Mary Ellison.

    d. She hallucinated under the influence of LSD.

18. Who were Amy Stallings's biological parents?

    a. Carol and Jay Stallings

    b. Jay Stallings and Natalie Hughes

    c. Natalie Hughes and Luke Porter

    d. Steve Andropolous and Andrea Korackas

19. What were the comical circumstances behind Margo Hughes's first meeting with Whit McColl?

    a. Just as he arrived in Oakdale and was about to introduce himself to Tom, Margo accidentally hit him with a shaving-cream pie, which she had meant for Tom.

    b. The minister who married Tom and Margo drove to the wacky outdoor ceremony in an ice cream truck, which rolled into Whit's limo during the proceedings.

    c. Margo cracked a prostitution ring and caught Whit blushingly pulling up his pants in a bimbo's bed.

    d. Whit arrived unexpectedly in Oakdale and sneaked into Lisa's bed, not realizing it was instead occupied by Margo; Margo assaulted him in self-defense, and he pressed charges.

AS THE WORLD TURNS

20. Which is not *true of the complex Karen Dixon?*

    a. She tried to steal Jeff away from Annie.

    b. She blackmailed James into marriage.

    c. She was engaged to David during his amnesia siege.

    d. She pursued Burke Donovan because she knew his son, Dustin, was to be an heir.

As the World Turns is a ratings winner thanks to lively, well-integrated storylines and an exciting array of young performers. Christian J. LeBlanc is featured as Kirk McColl, the rebellious youngest son of an authoritarian millionaire.

THE SOAP OPERA Digest SCRAPBOOK

As the World Turns Crossword Puzzle

ACROSS

1. Sharp punch
4. Singer Horne
8. Don Hastings = *ATWT*'s _____ Hughes
11. Beige
13. Roger _____ Brown = *DOOL*'s Danny Grant
14. *Name That* _____! (old TV musical quiz show)
15. Not foul; evenhanded
16. _____ = *ATWT*'s Craig Montgomery (full name)
18. Terri VandenBosch's *ATWT* role and others
20. Goes up
21. Title for Capitol's Mark Denning: Abbr.
22. Strange; uneven
23. _____ Anthony = *ATWT*'s Andy Dixon
25. "_____ Moon": Rodgers and Hart song
27. Kathy _____ = *ATWT*'s Karen Dixon
29. Patricia Bruder = *ATWT*'s _____ Stewart
31. Groups of cattle, sheep, etc.
32. _____ Jima, WWII battle site
35. _____ Russom = *ATWT*'s Zachary Stone

AS THE WORLD TURNS

36. Fountain drinks
37. Russian ruler, once; movie mogul
38. Marriage vow (two words)
39. Take _____ (vacation; two words)
40. Anne _____ = *ATWT*'s Lyla Montgomery
41. _____ Tomei = *ATWT*'s Marcy Thompson
43. Motel unit; space
44. Pile, such as wood, for burning
45. Lee Lawson = *GL*'s _____ Reardon
46. Taxi
49. *Soap* _____ *Digest*
52. See 29 Across
54. _____ = *ATWT*'s Gunnar Stenbeck (full name)
57. Natalie _____ = *AMC*'s Enid Nelson
58. Clothes presser
59. Abraham _____ = *GH*'s Alan, Jr.
60. _____ *Well That Ends Well*
61. They go with eithers
62. Russian news agency
63. Joe Morton = *AW*'s Abel Marsh/ _____ Mars

DOWN

1. Robert Lipton's *ATWT* role and others
2. Without _____ in the world (unworried; two words)
3. _____ = *ATWT*'s Dustin Donovan (full name)
4. Tied a shoe
5. God of love
6. He's _____ for her (evaluation of a marriage)
7. Picnic pest
8. Purchases
9. "_____ upon a time. . . ."
10. Honey makers
12. Coffee maker or holder
13. Stand _____ (move over)
14. Singer Lopez
17. Scottish hillsides
19. Part of speech (name, place or thing)
23. Fight; junk
24. Finishes; last words
26. Nickname for actor Nimoy or conductor Bernstein
27. TV, radio, newspapers, etc.
28. Betsy von Furstenberg = *ATWT*'s _____ (full name)
29. _____ Sims was *GL*'s Stephen Joyce
30. Showed the way; conducted
31. Dude ranch animal
33. _____ *and Peace*
34. Fort _____, California
36. Move; jail: Slang
37. "It Takes _____ to Tango"
39. Early Iranian
40. Fly high
42. Tied to one's _____ strings
43. Put on trial again
45. Boxers Max and Buddy
47. It leads to the altar
48. Deep voice
49. Columbus is its capital
50. Cat's happy sound
51. Psychological selves
52. Actress Zadora and newsperson Lindstrom
53. Author Levin
55. Actor's rep. or gov't. plainclothesman
56. Item in a pod

THE **SOAP OPERA** *Digest* SCRAPBOOK

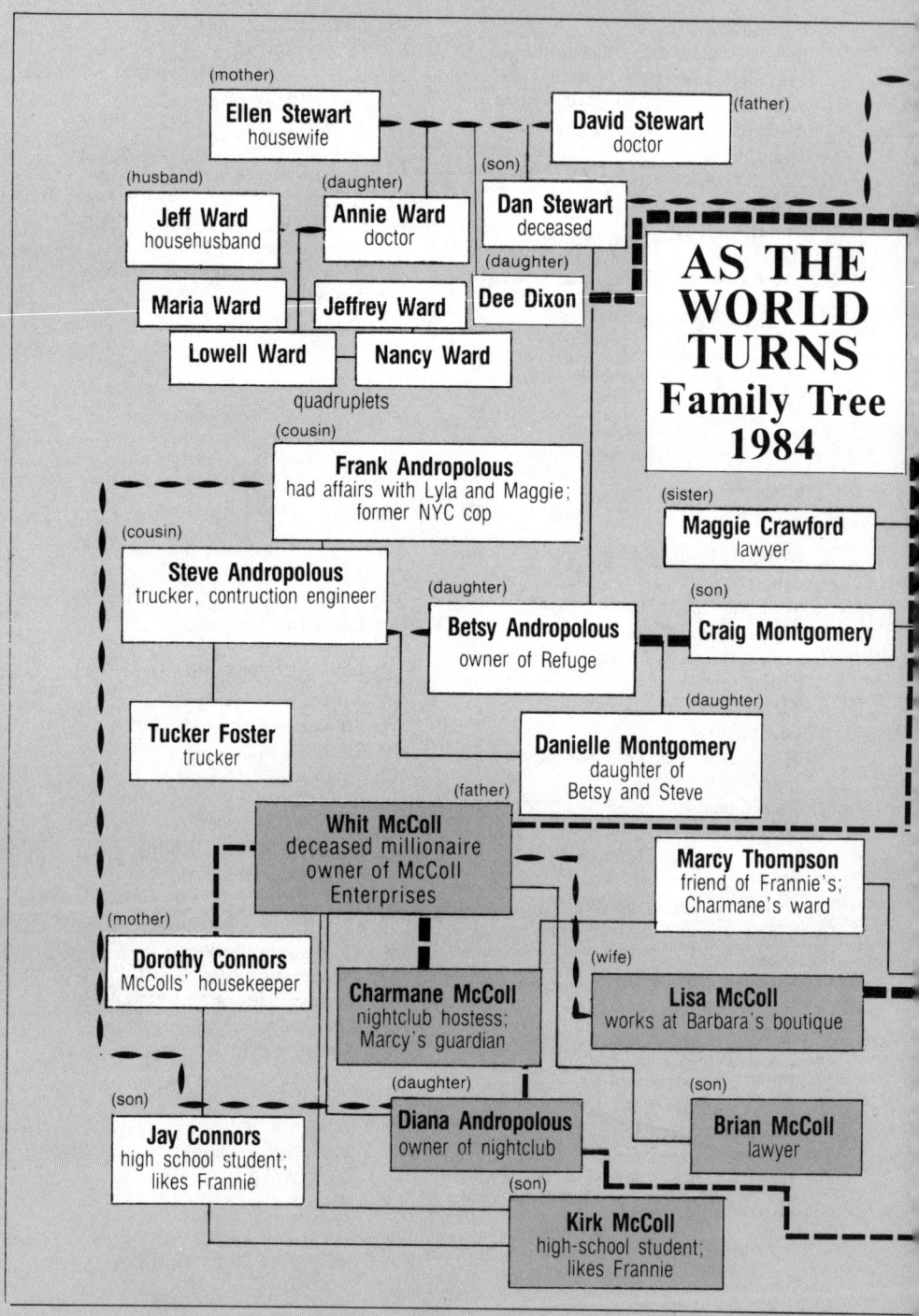

AS THE WORLD TURNS

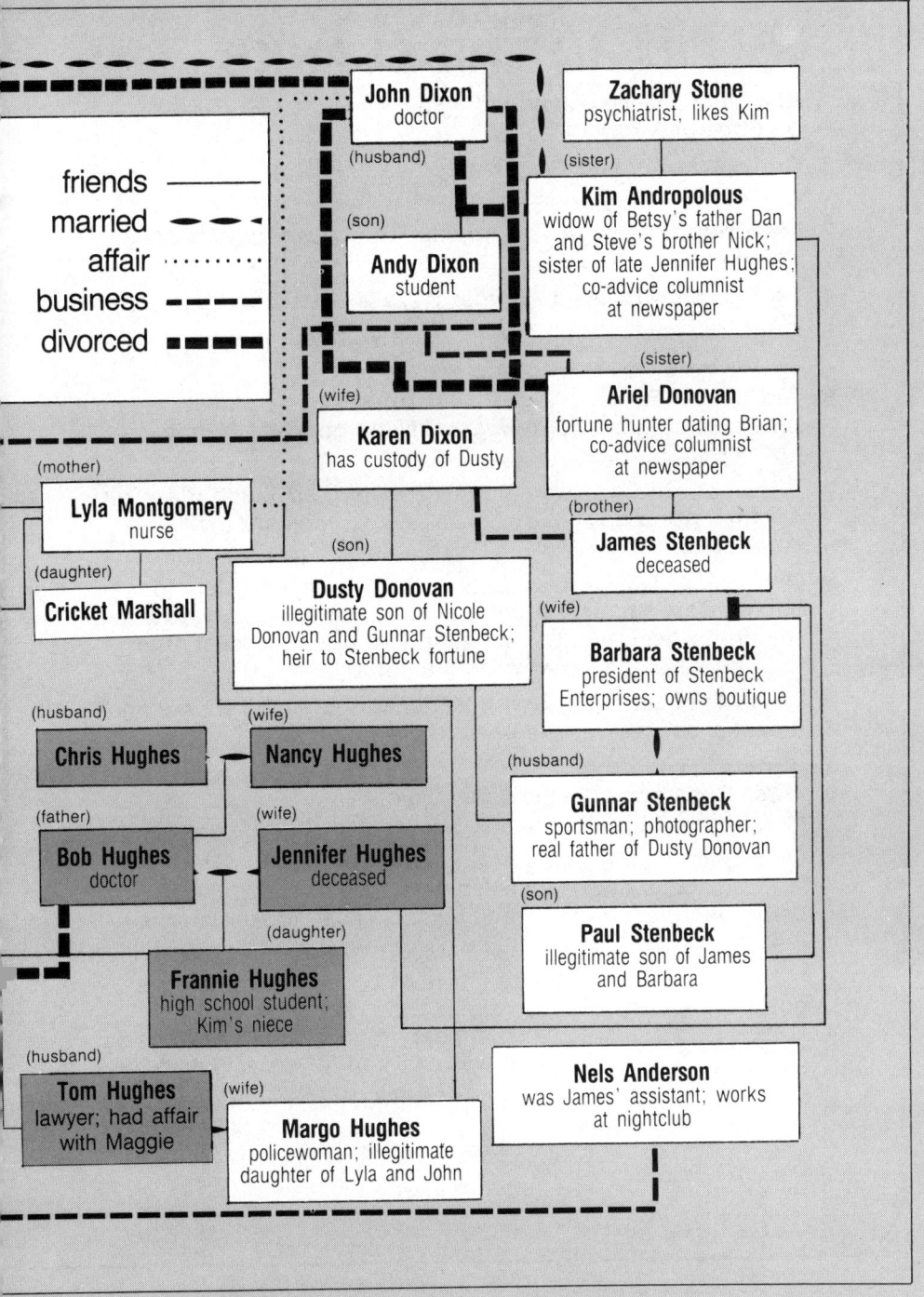

Soaptrivia #3
FILL IN THE BLANKS

1. Kim Hunter once played fading actress _____ on *Edge of Night*.
2. Carrie Wheeler and Greg Mercer were both reporters for the *Somerset* _____.
3. The original name of *The Haunted Star (General Hospital)* was the _____.
4. Leonie Norton played *Another World*'s _____.
5. Originally cast as *One Life to Live*'s Will Vernon was _____.
6. Teri Keane (Rose Donovan, *Loving*) previously played _____ on *Edge of Night* opposite Mandel Kramer as _____.
7. _____ created two soap roles, Mitch Blake on *Another World* and _____ Foster on *The Young and the Restless*.
8. On *Another World* _____ played Mac and Rachel Cory's housekeeper, _____, whose search for her daughter, Jennifer, led to the discovery that _____ was her granddaughter.
9. The entire cast of *General Hospital* attributes the show's phenomenal success to one person, producer _____.
10. Actor Christopher Reeve once played _____ on CBS's _____.
11. On *Capitol* Myrna Clegg arranged for a hooker, _____, to sleep with _____ before incriminating hidden cameras. That hooker later fell in love with _____.
12. In the prime-time premiere movie of *Loving* Lloyd Bridges guest-starred as _____, father of _____. Also appearing was Geraldine Page as _____, who was arrested for participation in a _____ ring.

13. On *Search for Tomorrow* Stu Bergman and his first wife, _____, had two children, _____ and _____. The latter was originally nicknamed _____.

14. On *Ryan's Hope* Rae Woodard and her daughter, _____, fought for the affections of _____, who had also impregnated Amy Morris, baby-sitter of _____.

15. *Guiding Light*'s Barbara Norris Thorpe had three children— _____, _____, and Holly.

16. Joan Crawford, Christina Crawford, Troy Donahue, and Audrey Landers all appeared on the defunct soap _____, which lasted for _____ years on CBS.

17. On *Love of Life* Bruce Sterling had two children, _____ and _____. He worked at the _____ Paper Company, taught at _____ Academy, and became principal of _____ High School.

18. The first several years of *The Young and the Restless* concerned Stuart Brooks, publisher of *The _____*, his wife _____, and his four daughters, _____, _____, _____, and _____.

19. On *Loving* Cabot and Isabelle Alden have two children, _____ and _____.

20. Roy Thinnes, Mark Hamill, Gary Frank, and Anne Jeffreys all played roles on _____.

Constance Towers (Clarissa McCandless)

4
CAPITOL

Twenty Questions

1. Which is not true of Clarissa McCandless and Myrna Clegg?

    a. They were best friends until Myrna's fiancé, Baxter McCandless, met and married Clarissa.

    b. They were raised by their feuding fathers to hate one another.

    c. Myrna ended the political career of Clarissa's father, Judson Tyler, by falsely implicating him during the Red Scare.

    d. Baxter McCandless was a lawyer who worked for Myrna's father.

2. The McCandlesses, the Cleggs, and the Dennings live in what Virginia suburb of Washington, DC?

    a. Alexandria
    b. Jeffersonia
    c. Newport News
    d. Richmond

THE SOAP OPERA *Digest* SCRAPBOOK

3. *What is Trey's status in the Clegg family?*

   a. He is Sam's son by his deceased first wife.
   b. He is Sam's son by his first wife, who is still alive.
   c. He was an orphan adopted by Sam and his deceased first wife.
   d. He was an orphan adopted by Sam and Myrna.

4. *How did Myrna Clegg try to put Phil Dade in her political pocket?*

   a. She had him videotaped with a hooker, Shelly Granger, who played dead and made it appear that Phil had killed her.
   b. She had him videotaped with a hooker, Shelly Granger, and threatened to show the tape to his wife, Joan.
   c. She had him drugged and photographed in bed with a hooker, Kelly Harper.
   d. She showed Joan Dade photos of Phil, Kelly, and Maggie Brady in a kinky *ménage à trois*.

5. *What were Lawrence Barrington's real name and occupation?*

   a. Gordon Waring; private detective
   b. Loring Hall; counterspy for the United States
   c. Warren Hull; industrial spy
   d. Gordon Hull; international spy

6. *Who carried a torch for Julie during her engagement to Tyler?*

   a. Wally McCandless   c. Kurt Voightlander
   b. Thomas McCandless   d. Lawrence Barrington

7. *Which was* not *true of the sleazy Danny Donato?*

   a. He turned out to be Ronnie Angelo's father.

CAPITOL

    b.   He owned the E-Z Rider bar.

    c.   He purchased Mario's restaurant.

    d.   He came upon Myrna's tape of Phil Dade.

8. Which one of these characters did away with slippery private eye Frank Burgess?

    a.   Kurt Voightlander   c.   Kelly Harper

    b.   Lawrence Barrington   d.   Phil Dade

9. What was Lisbeth Bachman when Jordy Clegg and Thomas McCandless began competing for her?

    a.   a beauty queen

    b.   a volunteer at Trey's campaign headquarters

    c.   a barmaid at the E-Z Rider

    d.   a sorority girl

Bill Beyers (Wally McCandless)

THE **SOAP OPERA** *Digest* SCRAPBOOK

10. *Why did Sloane pursue both Trey and Tyler?*

    a. She figured that, one way or the other, she would become first lady.

    b. She figured that, between the two of them, she could wangle promotions galore in the newscasting field.

    c. She wanted to anger her father enough that he would pay her the attention she felt she had been lacking.

    d. She wanted political secrets from both men so she could give them to Kurt Voightlander, but later she had a change of heart.

11. *What musical instrument does the reclusive Paula Denning play in her upstairs room?*

    a. violin   c. harpsichord

    b. chord organ   d. tuba

12. *What was Clarissa's relationship to Mark Denning at the time Tyler decided to enter politics?*

    a. They were platonic friends.

    b. They were bitter enemies.

    c. They were longtime lovers.

    d. They were friends on the surface, but Mark pressed her to acknowledge their mutual love.

13. *Through what means did Jordy discover that Amy Burke could have been fathered by Mark, Sam, or Baxter?*

    a. Myrna's flawless, compartmentalized memory

    b. a computer

    c. an admission that Fran Burke made to Jordy in confidence

    d. an admission that Sam made to Jordy in confidence

CAPITOL

14. How is Matt McCandless known on campus?

   a. He's not; he's studious and keeps a low profile
   b. as a conceited fool
   c. as a basketball star
   d. as a football hero

Capitol may be rife with vendettas and double-dealings in Washington, DC, but the love of Julie McCandless (Catherine Hickland) for her candidate husband still conquers all.

15. What is Ronnie's real first name?

   a. Veronica
   b. Rona
   c. Renata
   d. Ramona

16. How did Brenda Clegg try to win Wally's attention away from Ronnie?

   a. She swallowed a bottle of pills.
   b. She called him every day to profess her love.
   c. She hired a young man to pose as her boyfriend and make Wally jealous.
   d. She made it appear that Ronnie was having an affair with Ricky Driscoll.

THE SOAP OPERA Digest SCRAPBOOK

17. What was the name of Fran Burke's restaurant?

    a. E-Z Rider
    b. Swan Lake Grill
    c. Moon Lake Casino
    d. Twin Lakes Cafe

18. Who was Tyler's black right-hand man during the N'shoba crisis?

    a. Jeff Johnson
    b. Moses Jackson
    c. Joe Lucke
    d. Roscoe Jones

19. Why was Wally almost arrested for speeding?

    a. He was on his way to a card game to win back his gambling losses.
    b. He heard on the radio that there had been a shooting at the Denning house.
    c. He learned Brenda was on the brink of death at the hospital.
    d. Brenda told him that Ronnie and Zed were making time at Mario's.

20. Who was the housekeeper murdered by Paula Denning?

    a. Mrs. Mills
    b. Mrs. Miles
    c. Mrs. Billingsley
    d. Mrs. Millington

CAPITOL

Capitol Word Search

Soap-related words are hidden in this maze of letters. They read forward, backward, up, down, or diagonally, always in a straight line. Circle the letters as you find them. Letters may be used more than once. The remaining letters will (in order) spell a hidden message. To start, we have indicated the first word in bold type. Enjoy!

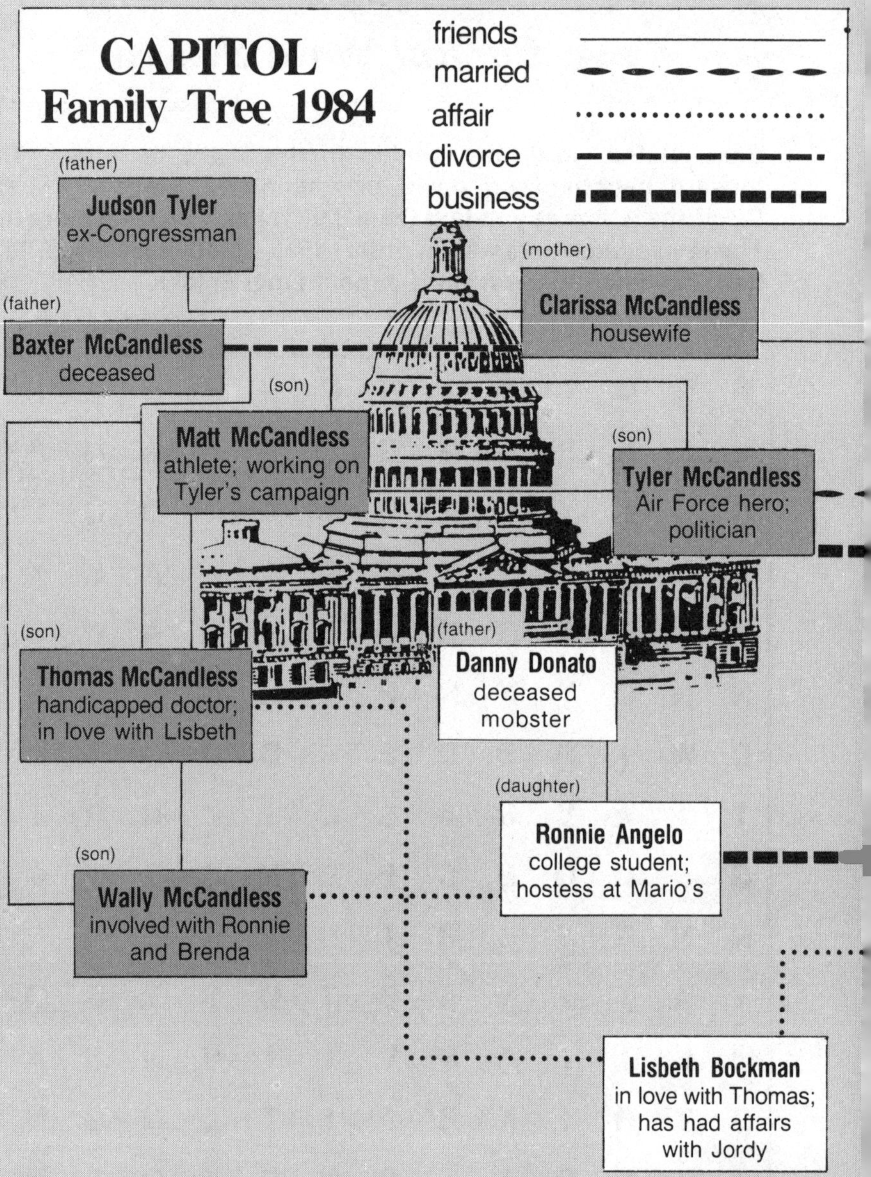

THE SOAP OPERA *Digest* SCRAPBOOK

CAPITOL Family Tree 1984

friends ─────
married ●●●●●
affair ·········
divorce ▬ ▬ ▬ ▬
business ▬▬▬▬

(father)
Judson Tyler
ex-Congressman

(mother)
Clarissa McCandless
housewife

(father)
Baxter McCandless
deceased

(son)
Matt McCandless
athlete; working on Tyler's campaign

(son)
Tyler McCandless
Air Force hero; politician

(son)
Thomas McCandless
handicapped doctor; in love with Lisbeth

(father)
Danny Donato
deceased mobster

(daughter)
Ronnie Angelo
college student; hostess at Mario's

(son)
Wally McCandless
involved with Ronnie and Brenda

Lisbeth Bockman
in love with Thomas; has had affairs with Jordy

CAPITOL

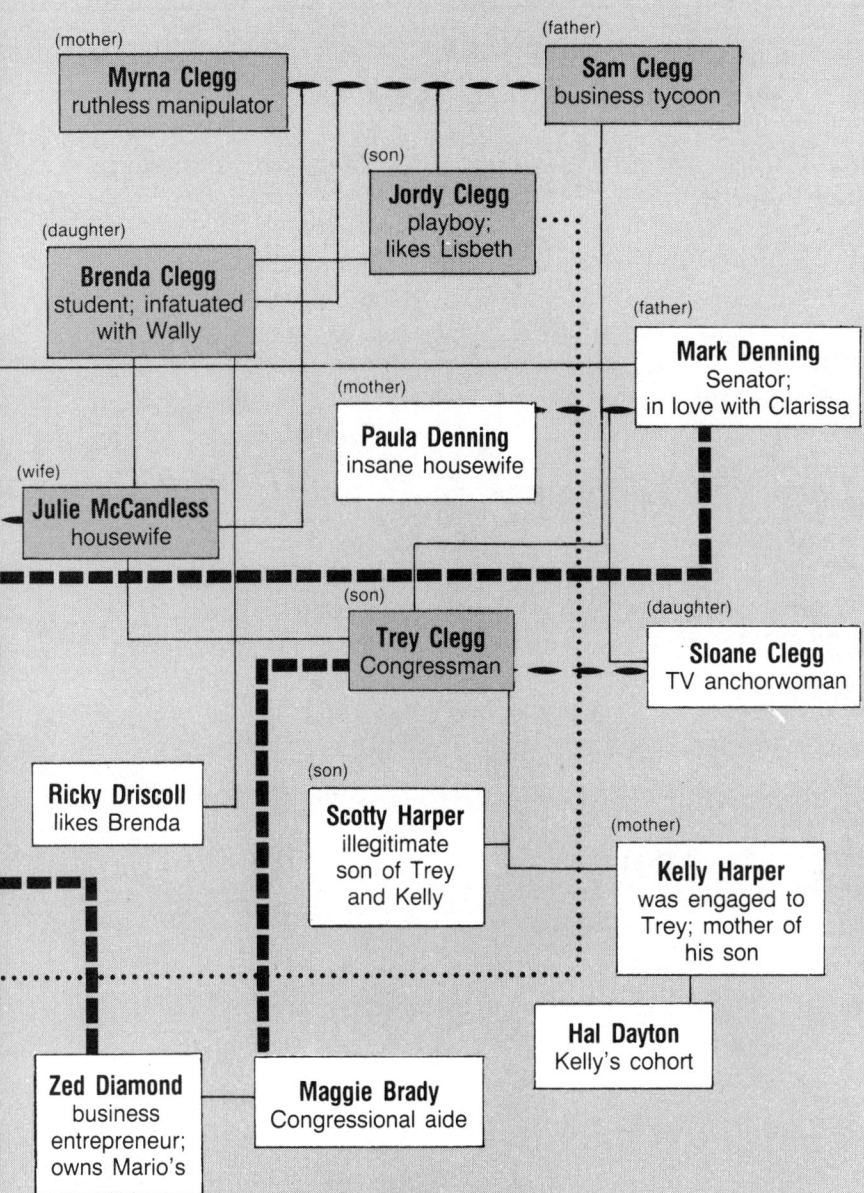

THE SOAP OPERA *Digest* SCRAPBOOK

Soaptrivia #4
WHAT A WAY TO GO

Match the following former soap characters with the way they met their demise.

A. Ted Clayton (*One Life to Live*)
B. Stephanie Martin (*Edge of Night*)
C. David Gray (*General Hospital*)
D. Roger Thorpe (*Guiding Light*)
E. Brian Kendall (*One Life to Live*)
F. Jennifer Brooks (*The Young and the Restless*)
G. Elizabeth Stewart (*As the World Turns*)
H. Garth Slater (*Loving*)
I. Alexandria Quartermaine (*General Hospital*)
J. Samantha Evans (*Days of Our Lives*)
K. Brandon Spaulding (*Guiding Light*)
L. Mary Matthews (*Another World*)
M. Dr. Tony Vincente (*Search for Tomorrow*)
N. Sara Fuller (*As the World Turns*)
O. Laura Hillyer (*Edge of Night*)
P. Dr. Lesley Webber (*General Hospital*)
Q. Bill Bauer (*Guiding Light*)
R. Kitty Tyler (*All My Children*)
S. Tracy Matthews (*Another World*)
T. Sara Karr (*Edge of Night*)

SOAPTRIVIA

1. Fell down a flight of stairs
2. Fell up a flight of stairs
3. Drove off a cliff
4. Had a sudden, massive heart attack
5. Strangulation
6. Stabbing
7. Was run over by a bus
8. Fell out of a window
9. Was pushed out of a window
10. Electrocution
11. Was frozen by an ice machine
12. Was run over by a car
13. Had a heart attack during a scuffle with criminals
14. Car accident
15. Cancer
16. Shooting
17. Fell off a cliff
18. Car explosion
19. Blood disorder
20. Had a heart attack when an enemy prevented the person from calling for help

Bill and Susan Seaforth Hayes (Doug and Julie Williams)

5
DAYS OF OUR LIVES

Twenty Questions

1. *Of the five Horton children, which two were fraternal twins?*

    a. Mickey and Bill
    b. Addie and Marie
    c. Addie and Tommy
    d. Tommy and Mickey

2. *What did Julie's father, Ben Olson, do for a living?*

    a. Nothing; he stayed home and drank while Addie supported him.
    b. He was an influential banker.
    c. He was a lawyer specializing in sensational civil cases.
    d. He was a criminal lawyer.

3. *Who were Susan Martin's long-estranged parents?*

    a. Diane and Richard Hunter
    b. Helen and John Martin
    c. Anna and Carl Sawyer
    d. Janet and Scott Banning

THE SOAP OPERA *Digest* SCRAPBOOK

4. *What emotional trauma led Marie to leave Salem and eventually become a nun?*

    a. She couldn't deal with her incestuous feelings toward her brother, Tommy, which had plagued her since childhood.

    b. She discovered that Mark Brooks, the amnesiac doctor she planned to marry, was her brother Tommy.

    c. Her fiancée, Mark Brooks, realized she had sexual yearnings for her brother, Tommy.

    d. Her brother Tommy drunkenly revealed that she was pregnant by Alex Marshall.

5. *To which one of the Hortons was Doug Williams first introduced, where did they meet, and what is Doug's actual name?*

    a. Bill Horton; University Hospital; Brent Williams

    b. Mickey Horton; a downtown saloon; Donato DiMera

    c. Addie Olson; Sergio's restaurant; Harvey Douglas

    d. Bill Horton; jail; Brent Douglas

6. *Why did Mickey Horton go insane?*

    a. He discovered that his son, Michael, was actually fathered by his brother, Bill.

    b. He learned he was sterile and that his father, Tom, had secretly arranged for Laura to conceive Mike through artificial insemination, for which Doug provided sperm.

    c. He realized Linda Patterson was lying about Melissa's being his daughter.

    d. He caught Mike and Melissa in bed, not yet realizing that neither was his child.

7. *Why did Susan's marriage to Greg Peters end in divorce?*

    a. Neil Curtis raped her in the park and impregnated her.

b. She realized she had been a willing victim when Greg's brother, Eric, raped her in the park.
   c. She learned he had provided sperm for Neil's artificial insemination experiment and indirectly fathered Rebecca North's child.
   d. Jack Clayton raped her in the park when he failed to violate his nubile stepdaughter, Trish.

8. What type of medical professional was Greg and Eric's father, Phil Peters?
   a. a veterinarian
   b. a neurosurgeon
   c. a quack who was nailed by Tom Horton for malpractice
   d. a cardiologist

9. What cheerful medic delivered a lot of babies in Salem?
   a. Neil Curtis
   b. Rusty Lincoln
   c. Mel Bailey
   d. Jordan Barr

10. For what deceased character was a University Hospital clinic named?
    a. Addie Williams
    b. Jack Clayton
    c. Bob Anderson
    d. David Martin

11. What song did Jeri Clayton sing to her daughter, Trish, in hopes that Trish would forgive her for a misunderstanding?
    a. "You're My Everything"
    b. "Side by Side"
    c. "The Men in My Little Girl's Life"
    d. "You and Me Against the World"

THE **SOAP OPERA** Digest SCRAPBOOK

12. *To what song did Doug and Julie give in to their first feelings of love?*

    a. "The Look of Love"   c. "Penthouse Serenade"
    b. "The Way We Were"   d. "I'm Just a Girl Who Can't Say No"

13. *Why did Phyllis Anderson shoot her daughter, Mary?*

    a. She discovered that Mary was why Alex threw her over.
    b. She mistook Mary for Julie, her intended victim.
    c. She mistook Mary for Brooke, her intended victim.
    d. She found Mary in bed with Neil.

14. *What was Brooke Hamilton's alias when she returned to Salem with a new face in order to fool everyone who believed her to be dead?*

    a. Leslie James   c. Stephanie Woodruff
    b. Cassie Burns   d. Lorie Masters

15. *When David Banning was presumed dead, why did Alice Horton refuse to attend the funeral?*

    a. She knew David was alive.
    b. She was incensed that Julie had feelings for Doug during his marriage to her mother, Addie.
    c. She was shocked at David's love for Valerie, a black girl.
    d. She wanted to stay by Mickey's side in the sanitarium.

16. *When Samantha Evans impersonated her sister, Marlena, in Salem, where did she stash Marlena?*

    a. in a seedy hotel room

DAYS OF OUR LIVES

    b.   in the basement of Doug's Place

    c.   in Bayview Sanitarium

    d.   in the secret passageway under the DiMera house

17. *Which one of these characters was* not *born illegitimately?*

    a.   Jennifer Rose Horton   c.   Donna Craig

    b.   Michael Horton   d.   David Banning

18. *Who was the real mother of Janice, Mickey and Maggie's adopted daughter?*

    a.   Linda Patterson   c.   Joanne Barnes

    b.   Brooke Hamilton   d.   Jean Barton

19. *Who are the parents of Roman, Kayla, and Bo Brady?*

    a.   Shawn and Helen   c.   Mike and Helen

    b.   Kevin and Cathleen   d.   Shawn and Caroline

20. *Which obscure family relationship is* not *true?*

    a.   Stefano DiMera fathered Renée Dumonde illegitimately, while his son Tony was actually fathered by another man.

    b.   Doug and Addie Williams fathered Hope, then Addie died and Doug married Addie's daughter Julie, making Julie both half-sister and stepmother to Hope.

    c.   Julie and Scott Banning conceived David out of wedlock, but Julie named him after David Martin, whom she initially believed to be the father.

    d.   Doug fathered Rebecca North's child, Dougie LeClair, through artificial insemination, but the child is legally that of Rebecca's ex-husband, Robert LeClair.

THE SOAP OPERA *Digest* SCRAPBOOK

Days of Our Lives Crossword Puzzle

ACROSS

1. Dog or cat
4. Richard _____ = *Capitol*'s Sam Clegg
8. Smoke and fog
12. _____ Bow, the "It" girl
14. Grace Garland = *AMC*'s _____
15. Some shows are recorded on _____
16. Andrew Masset = *DOOL*'s _____ (full name)
18. Portion of land
19. Stage actress Mary _____
20. Film actors Chaney, Sr. and Jr.
21. Sean Anthony = *ATWT*'s _____ Dixon
22. Samantha _____ = *DOOL*'s Noel Curtis
24. Gerald Anthony = *OLTL*'s _____ Dane
26. Sounds of hesitation
27. *DOOL*'s _____ Brady, played by 53 Across
29. *GH*'s Quartermaines, father and son
32. _____ of sole (boned sole)
33. Part of *AMC*
35. _____ Kaplan of *Welcome Back, Kotter*
36. _____ Reynolds is 31 Down
37. Iceberg
38. Part of *OLTL*
39. Solidarity members
40. TV-movie star Eve _____ (*Our Miss Brooks*)

DAYS OF OUR LIVES

41. Kristian Alfonso, Leann Hunley, or Gloria Loring
43. Opposite of SSW
44. Got up
45. Quinn _____ = *DOOL*'s Alex Marshall
49. Instrument for Rich or Krupa
50. Fibber
51. Miner's find
52. Starts an engine (with "up")
53. See 27 Across (full name)
56. Toward the sheltered side, at sea
57. "At _____!" (military order)
58. Dancer Alvin _____
59. Mark Tapscott was *Y&R*'s _____ Bancroft
60. Lead player
61. Health resort

DOWN

1. Fruit-peeling tool
2. Goof; make a mistake
3. *DOOL*'s Josh _____ (Chris Kositchek) and family
4. Straightens; levels
5. Stage-light filters
6. Curve; rainbow shape
7. Slangy turndown
8. Posture; way of standing
9. _____ Carey = *DOOL*'s Tom Horton
10. "Grand Ole _____"
11. It starts Gallison
12. Caveman's weapon
13. Dr. Zhivago's sweetheart
17. Smash hits; shouts of admiration
21. Lewis _____ = *AW*'s David Thatcher
23. Director _____ Clair
24. Bill Hayes, John Clarke, Jed Allen, etc.
25. God of war
27. Imitates; works like Marcel Marceau
28. South African lily
29. "Long _____ and Far Away"
30. _____ Turner = *FC*'s Jacqueline Perrault
31. See 36 Across (full name)
32. Untrue; unfaithful
34. Late comic Bruce, for short
36. _____ Gallison = *DOOL*'s Neil Curtis, and others
37. At no cost
39. High school or college dance
40. _____ Barber = *DOOL*'s Carrie Brady, and others
42. Last name of player of *DOOL*'s Melissa Anderson (see 50 Down)
43. Close by
45. Horseman
46. Cuddly Australian animal
47. Detective story author _____ Stanley Gardner
48. _____ on (depend on)
49. Fashion's Oscar _____ Renta (two words)
50. First name of 42 Down
52. Louise Shaffer was _____ Woodard (*RH*)
53. _____ Moines, Iowa
54. Have dinner
55. What jeans hug

THE SOAP OPERA Digest SCRAPBOOK

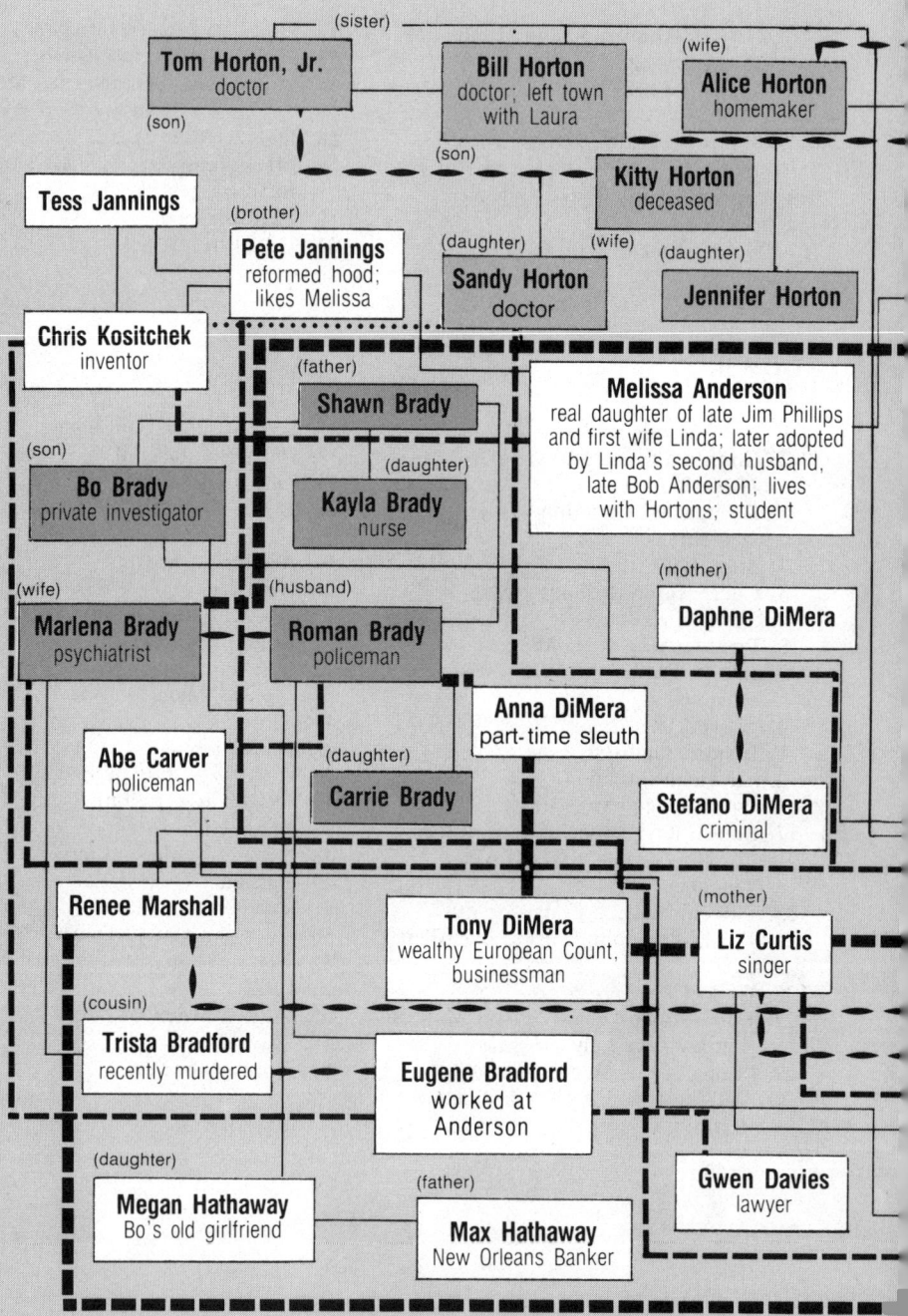

DAYS OF OUR LIVES

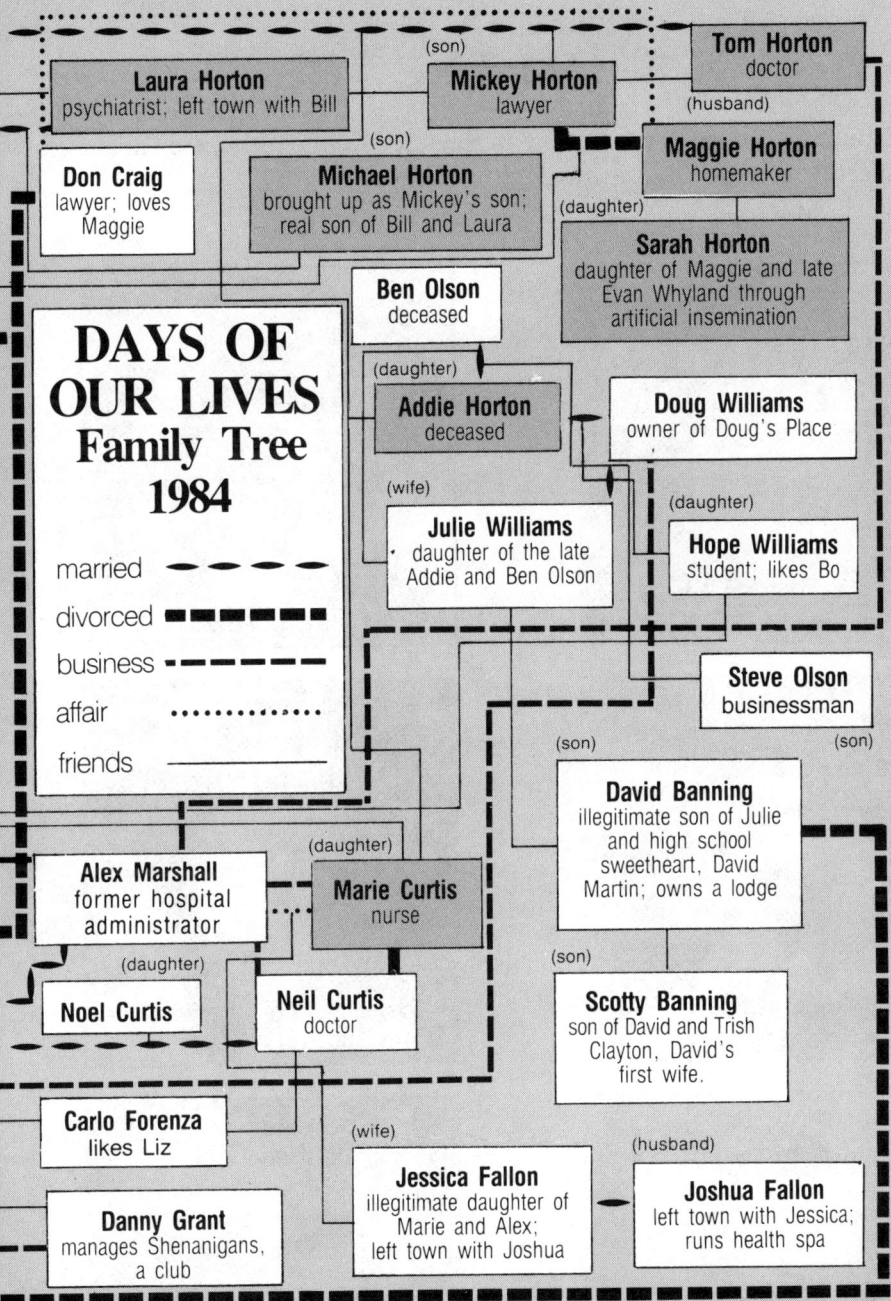

67

THE SOAP OPERA *Digest* SCRAPBOOK

Photoquiz #2
FAR FROM THE TREE

Match the on-screen offspring in the left column with his or her respective mom or dad in the right column.

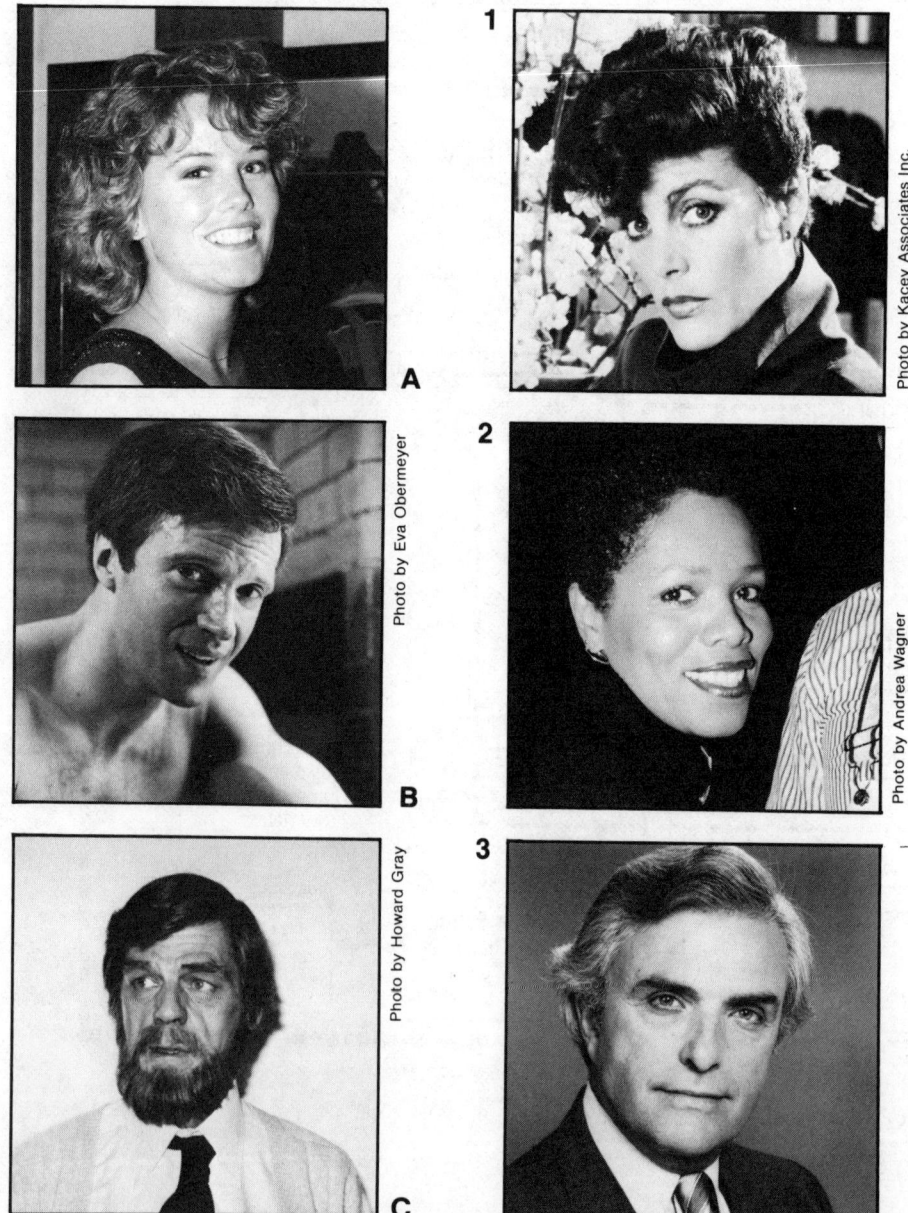

THE **SOAP OPERA** *Digest* SCRAPBOOK

A Question of Gender

Days of Our Lives didn't attract much audience notice at first, until Tommy Horton (John Lupton), the eldest Horton son, was introduced along with his wife, Kitty (Regina Gleason), and their daughter, Sandy (Heather North). Although Kitty had been mentioned in the first episode of the show, Tom and Alice (Macdonald Carey and Frances Reid) said at that time that Kitty had married their eldest son, *Danny*, and they had had a son, Bobby. Funny how Sandy never mentions her sex-change operation.

Pamela Roylance (Dr. Sandy Horton)

Soaptrivia #5
THEY HAD TO START SOMEWHERE

Match the current big-name star with the soap(s) that helped to launch his or her career.

A. Jill Clayburgh
B. Jameson Parker
C. Jessica Walter
D. Susan Sarandon
E. Donna Mills
F. Christopher Reeve
G. Ellen Burstyn
H. Hal Holbrook
I. Dick Van Patten
J. Jobeth Williams
K. Tommy Lee Jones
L. James Earl Jones
M. Tom Selleck
N. David Birney
O. Mark Hamill
P. Warren Beatty
Q. Kate Jackson
R. Larry Hagman
S. Patty Duke Astin
T. Cicely Tyson

1. *Love Is a Many Splendored Thing*
2. *The Doctors*
3. *The Brighter Day*
4. *General Hospital*
5. *Guiding Light*
6. *One Life to Live*
7. *Love of Life*
8. *As the World Turns*
9. *Search for Tomorrow*
10. *The Young and the Restless*
11. *Somerset*
12. *Dark Shadows*
13. *Edge of Night*
14. *A World Apart*
15. *The Secret Storm*
16. *Days of Our Lives*
17. *Ryan's Hope*
18. *Young Doctor Malone*
19. *Ryan's Hope*
20. *Another World*

Ann Flood (Nancy Karr)

6
EDGE OF NIGHT

Twenty Questions

1. Which was not *one of Mike Karr's jobs in his long crime-fighting career?*

    a. police chief
    b. police lieutenant
    c. defense attorney
    d. district attorney

2. Which couple never became the emotional victims of black-market baby sellers?

    a. Roger and Mary Harper
    b. Mike and Nancy Karr
    c. Bill and Martha Marceau
    d. Phil and Louise Capice

3. Which of these characters was not *a criminal?*

    a. Frank Dubeck
    b. Quentin Henderson
    c. Tony Saxon
    d. David Cameron

THE SOAP OPERA *Digest* SCRAPBOOK

4. *What was the endearing trademark of Winston Grimsley, the wealthy chairman of the Citizens' Crime Committee?*

   a. He held weekly sing-alongs at the Monticello Country Club.
   b. He had a passion for mystery novels.
   c. He had sherry every afternoon.
   d. He smoked fine cigars.

5. *Which character was a distant relative of Timmy Faraday, the little boy Mike and Nancy Karr adopted several years ago?*

   a. Nicole Cavanaugh
   b. Calvin Stoner
   c. Geraldine Saxon
   d. Derek Mallory

6. *On which picturesque island did Nancy uncover the dark secrets of Keith Whitney, Geraldine's maniacal son, and what did Keith put into Nancy's bed to scare her away?*

   a. Saint Eleanora; a scorpion
   b. San Carlos; a tarantula
   c. Eden; a boa constrictor
   d. San Angelo; a scantily clad, oversexed native

7. *Who was the attorney who married Nadine Alexander, Raven Whitney's now-deceased mother?*

   a. Adam Drake
   b. Ray Timmons
   c. Ansel Scott
   d. Vic Lamont

8. *Who was Derek Mallory's predecessor as chief of police, and what was his habit when he was baffled by a mystery surrounding a local crime?*

   a. Bill Marceau; eating a pound of linguine and clam sauce
   b. Bill Marceau; picking at his food at the dinner table

EDGE OF NIGHT

    c. Joe Pollock; watching baseball on TV
    d. Phil Capice; attending horse races

9. Which of these Monticello ladies has never been portrayed as a bitch?

    a. Mitzi Martin   c. Raven Whitney
    b. Deborah Saxon   d. Alicia Van Dine

10. Which of these classic villains was killed by someone holding a puppet?

    a. Eliot Dorn   c. Jefferson Brown
    b. Wade Meecham   d. Tony Saxon

**Forrest Compton
(Mike Karr)**

11. What was Adam Drake's profession before he became Mike's law partner and volunteer supersleuth?

    a. counterspy   c. private detective
    b. public defender   d. investigative reporter

THE SOAP OPERA Digest SCRAPBOOK

12. *What is the full name of Mike and Nancy's grandson, what is his nickname, and for whom was he named?*

    a. John Victor Dallas; "Johnny"; Johnny Dallas and Victor Carlson

    b. Victor Douglas Lamont; "Vic"; Vic Lamont

    c. John Victor Dallas; "J.V."; Johnny Dallas and Vic Lamont

    d. Philip Charles Lamont; "Chuckie"; Phil Capice

13. *Which description does not fit Eliot Dorn?*

    a. religious cult leader   c. actor
    b. restaurateur   d. puppeteer

14. *Who was the father of Nicole and Jody Travis, what was his legal front, and what was his criminal profession?*

    a. Orin Travis; district attorney; head of a loan shark ring

    b. Benjamin Travis; assistant to the governor; head of a loan shark ring

    c. Benjamin Travis; stockbroker; international counterspy

    d. Orin Hillyer; executive; secret owner of gambling casino

---

Lights, Camera, Whoops!

Edge of Night was a zany set in its early years, when it was live and starred John Larkin as Mike Karr. One day Larkin mistook air for dress rehearsal and fooled around by hurling funny obscenities at the stagehands. Finally one of them pointed to the red light on a camera, and Larkin learned the hard way how *not* to add humor touches to Mike Karr!

Edge of Night's Geraldine Whitney Saxon (Lois Kibbee) wields a lot of power in Monticello, but even she couldn't control the tragic fates of her family members. Her first husband and elder son were blasted to bits on a boat destroyed by mobsters, her younger son killed her brother and fell to his death from a landing, her daughter-in-law was shoved out of a window by a hit man who mistook her for someone else, and her second husband was shot by criminals in his employ. And this woman is still smiling!

Photo by Andrea Goldenberg

15. Which is an incorrect *match of wealthy employer and servant(s)?*

    a. Schuyler Whitney; Gunther Wagner

    b. Jefferson Brown; Bruno Wagner

    c. Geraldine Saxon; Ira and Vivian

    d. Geraldine Saxon; John and Trudy

16. What is Preacher Emerson's actual first name?

    a. John   c. Ralph

    b. Ken   d. Damien

17. What Monticello eatery has never been owned by a character on the show?

    a. The Coach House   c. The New Moon Cafe

    b. The Rock Garden   d. The Riverboat

Uh-Oh!

Harry Kramer had been *Edge of Night*'s announcer for at least 15 years when he one day intoned, "Stay tuned for the second half of *The Urge of Night!*"

18. Who was Eddie Lorimer's effervescent redheaded secretary, and with whom did she leave Monticello happily?

    a. Poppy Johnson; Spencer Varney
    b. Grace Endicott; Eddie Lorimer
    c. Grace Endicott; Damien Tyler
    d. Poppy Johnson; Damien Tyler

19. Who was Laurie Ann Karr's seldom-seen friend with whom she studied during her school years and who was named after the show's casting director of that time?

    a. Doreen Ackerman
    b. Whitney Voss
    c. Ruth Levine
    d. Joanne Goodhart

20. Geraldine Saxon's first husband, the deceased Gordon Whitney, proved an ineffectual weakling in what capacity?

    a. police commissioner
    b. governor
    c. senator
    d. cocaine smuggler

Edge of Night Word Search

Soap-related words are hidden in this maze of letters. They read forward, backward, up, down, or diagonally, always in a straight line. Circle the letters as you find them. Letters may be used more than once. The remaining letters will (in order) spell a hidden message. To start, we have indicated the first word in bold type. Enjoy!

```
I  M  A  G  E  I  N  K  Y  R  E  T  S  Y  M
N  I  I  R  V  I  N  G  A  L  L  E  N  O  O
O  L  T  F  I  W  S  N  A  G  O  L  N  A  T
X  E  T  T  K  F  S  I  V  A  R  T  S  Y  H
A  S  P  R  E  A  C  H  E  R  I  S  H  R  E
S  C  T  E  R  I  H  S  E  C  N  H  A  O  R
E  A  S  N  R  S  E  I  E  D  O  E  R  L  H
N  V  E  O  Y  O  D  L  G  S  S  L  O  L  O
I  A  R  T  R  N  L  B  S  S  A  L  N  A  O
D  N  R  S  E  O  O  U  R  J  E  G  M  D
L  A  O  I  O  Y  R  P  K  F  O  Y  A  K  D
A  U  F  D  D  U  M  I  T  Z  I  R  B  E  O
R  G  S  I  E  A  N  Z  T  N  A  G  E  R  O
E  H  A  D  C  H  R  I  S  Y  T  S  T  E  L
G  U  N  T  H  E  R  W  A  G  N  E  R  D  F
```

81

THE SOAP OPERA *Digest* SCRAPBOOK

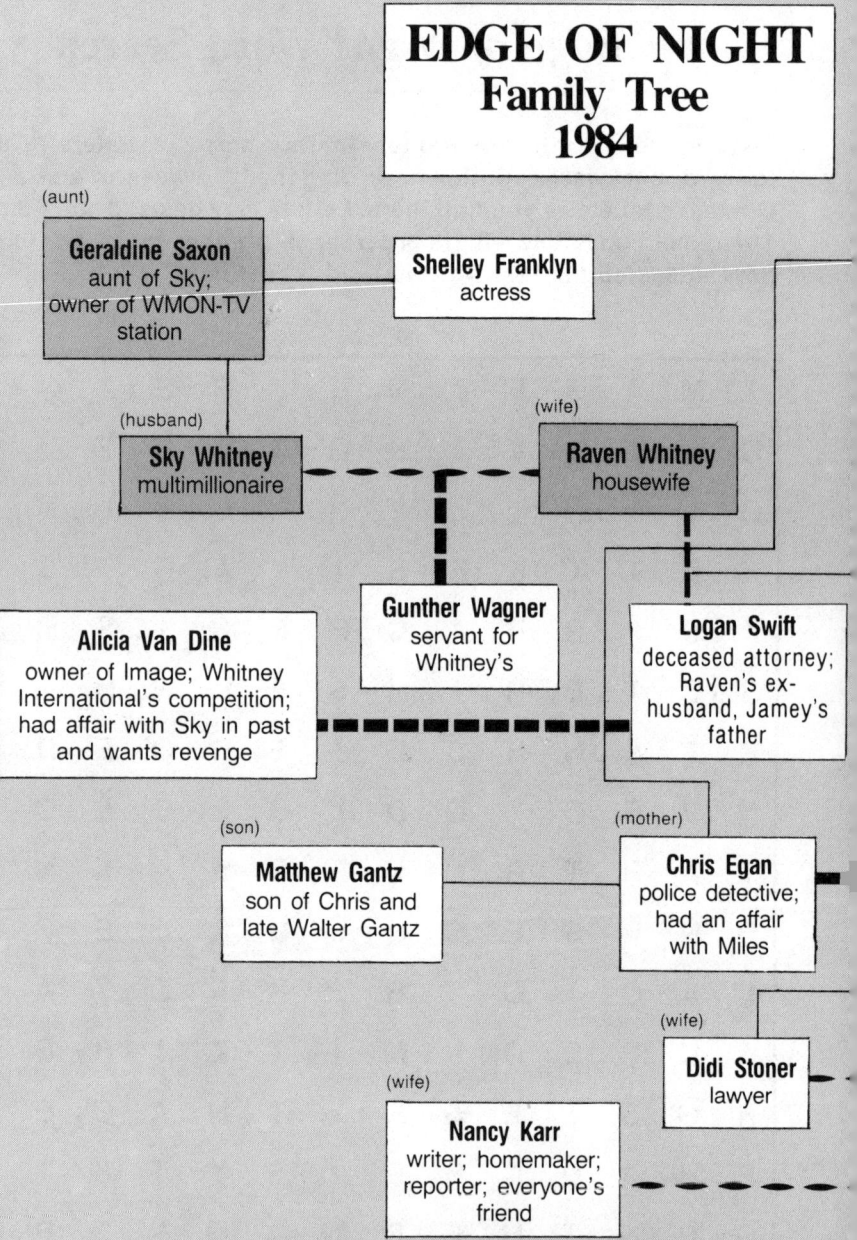

EDGE OF NIGHT

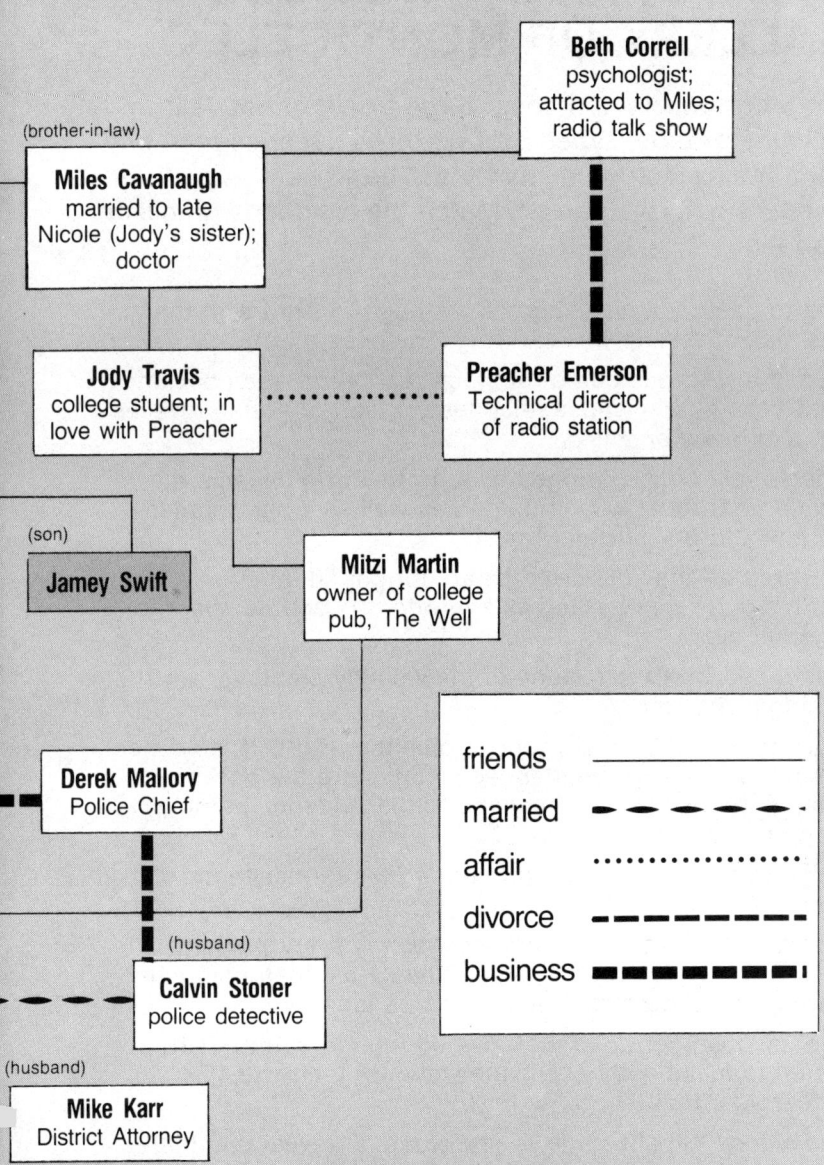

Soaptrivia #6
THE OFFICIAL ROGUES' GALLERY OF MONTICELLO

Being a crime-oriented soap, *Edge of Night* has featured more villains of more types over its three decades than any other fictionalized story in any form. The 10 nasties pictured are a mere drop in the bucket. Match the evildoer with his or her misdeed.

1. Tried to destroy Draper Scott's marriage to April with the false claim that she was carrying Draper's child
2. Headed a religious cult of dubious reputation, then became a heartless gigolo whose relentless pursuit of young lovelies won him many enemies.
3. Impersonated his estranged twin brother and became the servant to another wily impostor, as well as a blackmailer and a would-be statutory rapist
4. Appeared on the surface to be an upright counterespionage agent, only to be revealed as a murderous double agent for the other side
5. Absconded with the fortune of the wealthy employer who had long trusted him
6. Intended to murder her friend's romantic rival with poisoned tea, only to have an unintended victim slurp the potion instead, then killed the man who found evidence pointing to her guilt
7. Conducted spy activities and married his former friend's lover
8. Impersonated and stole from the wealthy friend he had mistakenly left for dead after a plane crash, then committed a string of murders to conceal his true identity
9. Acted as the agent of a mob-owned foreign country who plotted to make Jody Travis the victim of a bizarre, murderous ritual
10. Held Nancy Karr hostage so she wouldn't reveal that his boss, a plastic surgeon, altered the faces of wanted criminals to render them unrecognizable to the authorities

Peter Hansen (Lee Baldwin)

Susan Brown (Dr. Gail Baldwin)

7
GENERAL HOSPITAL

Twenty Questions

1. What song played in the background when Luke raped Laura, and who was the featured performer on the recording?

    a. "Theme From Flashdance"; Irene Cara
    b. "American Pie"; Don McLean
    c. "Rise"; Herb Alpert
    d. "New York, New York"; Frank Sinatra

2. What was Dr. Steve Hardy's unique background before he joined the staff of General Hospital?

    a. He was a professional baseball player.
    b. He was raised in China by his American missionary parents.
    c. He ran a resort in the Italian Catskills.
    d. He was a millionaire playboy who wanted a direction in life.

3. Who is the long-deceased mother of Scotty Baldwin?

    a. Meg Bentley   c. Peggy Mercer
    b. Brooke Clinton   d. Augusta McLeod

4. Who were the three student nurses terrorized daily by nurse Lucille March at the nurses' station?

    a. Guarnieri, Pastor, and Shaw
    b. Laird, Sogard, and Palumbo
    c. Williams, Chamberlain, and McGillis
    d. McGillis, McBride, and Clampett

5. Which two men served as administrators of General Hospital?

    a. Howard Dawson, Dan Rooney
    b. Henry Pinkham, Dan Rooney
    c. Arnold Thurston, Charles Lutz
    d. Arnold Thurston, Dan Rooney

6. What dread disease did Jeremy Hewitt spread to the people of Port Charles?

    a. lhasa fever   c. herpes
    b. yellow fever   d. crab lice

7. What is the chronic illness that plagues Lee Baldwin?

    a. arthritis   c. bursitis
    b. alcoholism   d. heartburn

8. What is Bobbie Spencer's full name?

    a. Barbara Jean Spencer   c. Roberta Jean Spencer
    b. Roberta Ann Spencer   d. Bobette Jean Spencer

General Hospital's young characters are usually at loose ends, but Bryan Phillips (Todd Davis) is always a stabilizing influence. A reformed alcoholic and AA representative, he dedicates much of his time to helping others while his shallow heiress wife snaps up pricey threads at chic local shops.

Photo by Kacey Associates Inc.

9. What blunt object was used to kill Phil Brewer?

    a. knife   c. geode

    b. stone   d. baseball bat

10. Which of these four medics never specialized in cardiac medicine?

    a. Jim Hobart   c. Rick Webber

    b. Tom Baldwin   d. Mark Dante

11. Which is the correct order of Jessie Brewer's husbands?

    a. John Prentice, Phil Brewer, Phil Brewer

    b. Phil Brewer, John Prentice, Phil Brewer

    c. Al Weeks, John Prentice, Phil Brewer

    d. John Prentice, Phil Brewer, Peter Taylor

THE SOAP OPERA *Digest* SCRAPBOOK

12. *Who is Laura's natural father?*

    a. Rick Webber   c. Al Weeks
    b. Lars Webber   d. Gordon Grey

13. *Which couple raised Laura as their own when Lesley believed her to be dead?*

    a. Emma and Charlie Lutz
    b. Barbara and Jason Vining
    c. Barbara and John Vining
    d. Janet and Fred Fleming

14. *Where did Audrey hide her gun when she was wrongly accused of killing Peggy Nelson, her blackmailing baby nurse?*

    a. in her toilet tank
    b. in a wall safe
    c. in a toolbox she stole from Al Weeks
    d. in her kitchen cabinet

15. *Who was the landlady who arranged to put Heather's son, Steven Lars, on the black market?*

    a. Clare Steele   c. Edna Hamilton
    b. Edna Hadley   d. Edith Lyons

16. *What is the profession of Noah Drake's uncle, Martin Drake?*

    a. senator   c. history teacher
    b. oil magnate   d. restaurateur

17. *Who was the rejecting lover Laura killed in a fit of passion?*

    a. Darren Blythe   c. Gary Lansing
    b. David Hamilton   d. Julian Drake

GENERAL HOSPITAL

18. What is the name of Rick and Jeff Webber's elder sister, and what is her line of work?

   a. Helene Webber; nurse
   b. Mary Ellen Lowell; nightclub singer
   c. Meg Bentley; nurse
   d. Terri Arnett; nightclub singer

19. What was the familial relationship between Rose and Joe Kelly?

   a. He was her stepson.
   b. He was her husband.
   c. He was her brother.
   d. none

Exile at Mercy Hospital

In soaps anything can happen. Within several months during the mid-70's *General Hospital* had two characters turn up who were presumed dead—Rick Webber (in Africa) and Tom Baldwin (in Mexico). But not long before, several long-running characters were terminated when headwriters transferred them to nearby Mercy Hospital, and they were never heard from again. Obviously the worst fate for a *GH* character is not death but a stint at Mercy!

20. What was the name of Heather's roommate at the sanitarium?

   a. Sara Lane   c. Shelly Vernon
   b. Beth Maynard   d. Sarah Abbott

THE SOAP OPERA Digest SCRAPBOOK

General Hospital Crossword Puzzle

ACROSS

1. Printed commercials
4. Film's _____ Ray
8. Susan Lucci = AMC's Erica _____ Chandler
12. Confess
14. _____ Russom = ATWT's Zachary Stone
15. Grandson of Adam: Bible
16. _____ Northrup = DOOL's Roman Brady
17. "_____ of Capri": 1934 song
18. Field laborer; peasant
19. Letter holder: Abbr.
20. Fred and _____ Astaire
22. _____ Caudell was DOOL's Woody King
23. Illinois U.'s football team, the Fighting _____
25. Richard _____, lead in An Officer and a Gentleman
26. GH's _____ Roskov, and others
28. _____ Perry Scott = Nels Anderson (ATWT)
31. In case; as though (two words)
32. Todd Davis, David Walker, or Jack Wagner
33. TV's "_____ Na Na"
36. The #1 soap
40. Droop
41. _____ Patrick Clarke = GH's Grant Andrews

42. Recite; explain
43. Smarter; more intelligent
44. Gives up claim to; relinquishes legally
46. Rachel _____ = *GH*'s Audrey Hardy
48. _____ Bishop = *GH*'s Rose Kelly
50. Chunk of meat or metal
51. Grizzlies
52. Lee Lawson = *GL*'s _____ Reardon
55. Anthony Call = *OLTL*'s _____ Callison

56. Stephen Schnetzer = *AW*'s _____ Winthrop
57. Michael _____ = *GL*'s Jim Reardon
59. "Perry Mason" author, _____ Stanley Gardner
60. Orchestra instrument
61. Sandy Gabriel's *AMC* role and others
62. A _____ Is Born
63. Writing tools
64. Hair color

DOWN

1. Shell (8 Down) = *GH*'s _____ (full name)
2. *Gunga* _____: 1939 film
3. _____ kiss (flirt, in a way; two words)
4. E.T., for one
5. She's *GH*'s Monica Quartermaine (full name)
6. _____ out (apportion)
7. Part of *OLTL*
8. See 1 Down
9. Lend _____ (listen; two words)
10. Kathleen _____ = *AMC*'s Ellen Dalton
11. Ancient slave
12. Wonder; amazement
13. Frank Maxwell = *GH*'s _____ Rooney
21. Prefix for aster, may, and mal
24. Part of OLTL
25. *The World According to* _____
26. Labels
27. On the ocean
29. "let's get _____!" ("let's do it!"; two words)

30. Numbers: *Abbr.*
32. "It's a sin to (42 Across) _____"
33. _____ = *GH*'s Jimmy Lee Holt (full name)
34. Ron _____ = *RH*'s Roger Coleridge
35. "_____ Well That Ends Well"
37. Batter's statistic: *Abbr.*
38. "_____ gratia artis" M-G-M's motto
39. Put _____ writing (give written proof; two words)
43. David Mendenhall = *GH*'s Mike _____
44. "Make love, not _____"
45. Question and _____ period
46. Warning; signal; ready
47. _____ Adams = *Y&R*'s Dina Abbott
49. Desert paradises
50. "_____ too fat for me" (from "Too-Fat Polka")
51. Home-run slugger, _____ Ruth
53. Columnist _____ LeShan
54. Dolt; wimp; nerd
56. *SFT*'s Brian Emerson, for one
58. Poetic form

THE SOAP OPERA *Digest* SCRAPBOOK

GENERAL HOSPITAL
Family Tree 198[4]

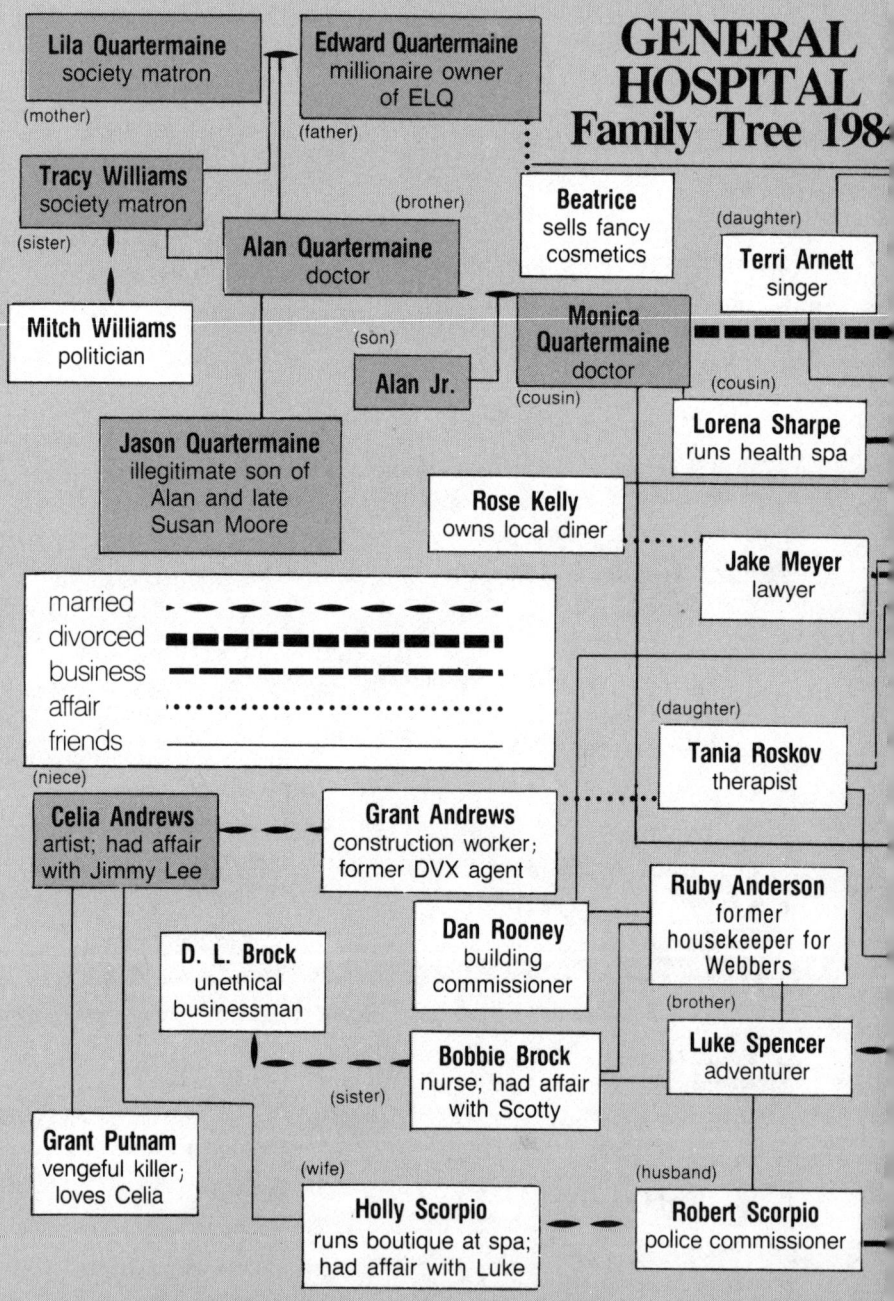

GENERAL HOSPITAL

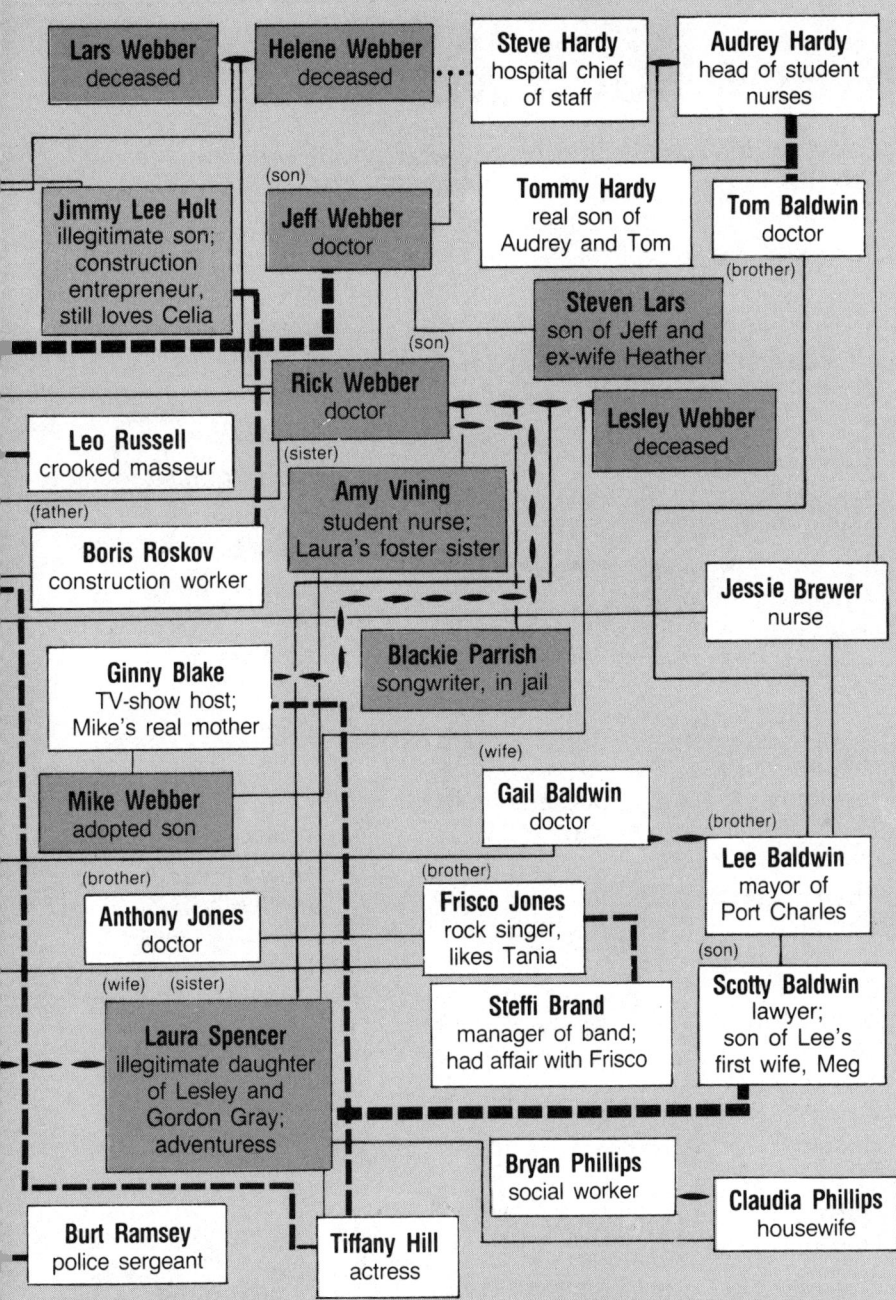

THE SOAP OPERA *Digest* SCRAPBOOK

Soaptrivia #7
HOW SOON WE FORGET

Many serials have fallen by the proverbial wayside. Here are 20 titles no longer gracing the weekly TV listings. Match the title with its correct theme and group of featured performers.

A. Love of Life
B. The Secret Storm
C. The Brighter Day
D. From These Roots
E. Young Doctor Malone
F. The Clear Horizon
G. The Doctors
H. Dark Shadows
I. Love Is a Many Splendored Thing
J. Where the Heart Is
K. A World Apart
L. Somerset
M. Return to Peyton Place
N. How to Survive a Marriage
O. Texas
P. Valiant Lady
Q. Bright Promise
R. For Richer, For Poorer
S. Flame in the Wind
T. The Nurses

1. The longtime residents of Bancroft, a college town
2. The families of a small Michigan town supported largely by a frozen-food firm
3. The staff of Alden General Hospital
4. The staff of Hope Memorial Hospital
5. The staff of Valley Hospital
6. Class conflict in the town of Haviland
7. Sex and sin in the town of Northcross
8. The large family of a widowed minister
9. Creepy doings in the Collingwood mansion
10. A large, somewhat neurotic family that owned a department store and a newspaper
11. New England family that owned a newspaper
12. Families involved with the oil industry
13. Air corps staff and their families in Cape Canaveral
14. The widow and three children of an inventor

96

SOAPTRIVIA

Dr. Jekyll or Mr. Hyde?

NBC's *The Doctors* once featured the popular character of Jerry Dancy (Jonathan Hogan), a hardworking, idealistic young lawyer from a struggling family. He left the show, only to return a few years later—as an unethical *doctor*!

15. Class conflict in the town of Point Claire

16. Star-crossed romance of an ingenue and an unhappily married heir

17. Two sisters— one good, one amoral

18. Three families in Chicago

19. Three families in San Francisco

20. The women of Lakeview

a. James Mitchell, Louise Shaffer, Delphi Harrington, David Cryer

b. Gloria Hoye, Hal Holbrook, Blair Davies, Lois Nettleton

c. Gloria Hoye, Joel Crothers, Bibi Besch, Paul Sparer

d. Joel Crothers, Alexandra Moltke, Joan Bennett, Jerry Lacy

e. Audrey Peters, Ron Tomme, Jerry Lacy, Tudi Wiggins

The Show Must Go On

Minutes before air time on NBC's *From These Roots*, director Paul Lammers had a verbal exchange with a temperamental actress who took it upon herself to quit her role at that precise moment. Lammers had no choice but to plop his script girl into a chair before the cameras to read the actress's lines directly from the script!

f. Rod Arrants, Christine Jones, Richard Backus, Patricia Barry

g. William Prince, Augusta Dabney, Stephen Elliott, Robert Gentry

h. William Prince, Augusta Dabney, Stephen Elliott, Judson Laire

i. Judson Laire, Gloria Hoye, Augusta Dabney, Albert Stratton

j. Judson Laire, Mary Fickett, Sally Gracie, Nat Polen

k. Jada Rowland, James Pritchett, Wayne Tippit, Sally Gracie

l. Jada Rowland, James Pritchett, Wayne Tippit, Haila Stoddard

m. Susan Brown, Dabney Coleman, Tony Geary, Anne Jeffreys

n. Susan Brown, Yale Summers, Katherine Glass, Joseph Gallison

o. Edward Kemmer, Denise Alexander, William Roerick, Ted Knight

p. Josephine Nichols, Roy Poole, Jane Elliot, Conard Fowkes

q. Josephine Nichols, Jerry Lanning, Carla Borelli, Jay Hammer

r. Robert Mandan, Billie Lou Watt, Len Wayland, Audra Lindley

s. Flora Campbell, James Kirkwood, Jr., Martin Balsam, John Graham

t. Joan Copeland, Steve Elmore, Jennifer Harmon, Michael Landrum

The Ultimate Ad Lib

On NBC's *Young Doctor Malone* a noncontract character actor played a caretaker who had to knock on a door and deliver some information to Matt Steele (Nicolas Coster) and Erika Brandt (Ann Williams). The character man drew a total blank and hemmed and hawed. This being live television, Coster and Williams then had the task of telling the caretaker why he had knocked on their door!

Geronimo!

When NBC briefly brought radio's popular *One Man's Family* to daytime television, Ralph Locke and Mona Bruns played a married couple who had a scene on an airplane. Locke, a seasoned radio actor unaccustomed to the demands of television, went "sky high" on his lines and excused himself by saying, "I'm afraid this is my stop." Obviously *One Man's Family* was the forerunner of *Ripcord*!

Truly one of the great ladies of daytime television, Lori March played "bitch goddesses" on *Three Steps to Heaven* and *The Brighter Day*, but on *The Secret Storm* she played heroic, understanding stepmother Valerie Hill Ames.

Charita Bauer (Bert Bauer)

8
GUIDING LIGHT

Twenty Questions

1. Which one of these men never married Meta Bauer?

    a. Mark Holden
    b. Ted White
    c. Joe Roberts
    d. Bruce Banning

2. What was Papa Bauer's line of work?

    a. He owned a saloon.
    b. He had a farm.
    c. He was a carpenter.
    d. He was the Cedars Hospital custodial staff chairman.

3. Meta's stepdaughter, Kathy, was the mother of Robin, a confused girl who grew up searching for a strong male figure in her life. Who was Robin's real father, who was the man Kathy alleged to be her father, and who was her adoptive father?

    a. Dick Grant; Mark Holden; Bruce Banning

b. Bob Lang; Dick Grant; Paul Fletcher
c. Bob Lang; Dick Grant; Mark Holden
d. Ted White; Mark Holden; Dick Grant

4. Bert Bauer was at one time a dominating mother who annulled one of her sons' marriages to a girl and helped push the girl into a disastrous marriage to a vain older man. Which is the correct triangle Bert helped to perpetuate?

    a. Ed Bauer–Leslie Jackson–Stanley Norris
    b. Ed Bauer–Holly Norris–Adam Thorpe
    c. Mike Bauer–Julie Conrad–George Hayes
    d. Mike Bauer–Robin–Alex Bowden

5. Why did wealthy Henry Benedict try to win custody of his grandson, John Fletcher, from his son-in-law, Dr. Paul Fletcher?

    a. Paul and John lived in a rough section of town.
    b. John was distraught over Paul's impending marriage to Robin.
    c. Paul was having an affair with Doris Crandall.
    d. John was neglected by his nanny, Paul's half-sister, Jane.

6. Who was Mike Bauer's second father figure, boss, and legal mentor?

    a. Alex Bowden   c. Mark Holden
    b. George Hayes   d. Ben Scott

7. Who mothered Mike's daughter, Hope, and what ultimately happened to her?

    a. Robin; murdered
    b. Robin; run over by a car
    c. Julie; died in a mental institution
    d. Julie; drowned in a pool

GUIDING LIGHT

8. Which was not *true of Charlotte, the most evil of Mike Bauer's wives?*

   a. She posed as Tracy Delmar, Sara McIntyre's niece.
   b. She married John Fletcher because Henry Benedict gave him a large trust fund at age 21.
   c. She married Paul Fletcher for his money and status.
   d. She had a sordid past with criminal Marty Dillman.

9. Which of these characters was not *an artist?*

   a. Marie Grant
   b. Anne Fletcher
   c. Joe Turino
   d. Ben McFarren

10. Throughout Bert Bauer's long marriage to Bill he had a variety of jobs and mistresses. He once had an affair with his lonely secretary, which initially destroyed her daughter. What is the correct combination of job, secretary, and daughter?

    a. Public relations, Maggie Scott, Peggy Scott
    b. Insurance, Maggie Scott, Peggy Scott
    c. Car sales, Simone Kincaid, Hillary Kincaid
    d. Public relations, Simone Kincaid, Hillary Kincaid

11. What was Dr. Steve Jackson's position at Cedars Hospital?

    a. chief of surgery
    b. chief of cardiac surgery
    c. chief of internal medicine
    d. chief of staff

12. Steve's daughter, Leslie, hastily married the wealthy Stanley Norris in between her marriages to brothers Ed and Mike Bauer. Leslie was tried unjustly for the murder of the womanizing Norris. Who really murdered him and why?

    a. Linell Conway; he rudely rebuffed her sexual advances.

b. Marion Conway; he hurt her daughter Linell.

c. Kit Vested; he had dumped her for Leslie.

d. David Vested; he had fired David and hired Roger Thorpe.

13. *Which one of these women has had two husbands who tried to kill her?*

    a. Leslie Bauer   c. Charlotte Bauer

    b. Meta Bauer   d. Sara McIntyre

14. *How did Barbara Norris, Stan's ex-wife, make a good enough living to rear her three children?*

    a. She ran a restaurant.

    b. She wrote a cooking column.

    c. She had a TV cooking show.

    d. She ran the Cedars Hospital cafeteria.

15. *Why did Jackie Marler give up her son, Phillip, at the clinic where he ended up in the hands of Alan and Elizabeth Spaulding?*

    a. She was single and didn't want Justin to think she was trapping him into marriage.

    b. She had been engaged to Justin but realized he only wanted to rub noses with her famous surgeon father.

    c. She was married to Justin, who told her he hated children.

    d. She was married to Justin but figured her marriage was over because she caught him in bed with someone else.

16. *How did Roger blackmail Alan?*

    a. He discovered that Alan had bribed a witness to claim falsely that he and Elizabeth had had an affair in Madrid.

    b. He photographed Alan in a clinch with Diane Ballard during his marriage to Jackie.

c. While hiding on a remote island from the authorities, he saw Alan and Hope making love on the beach and realized Alan was cheating on Jackie.

d. He paid Dr. Paul Lacrosse for a sworn affidavit stating that Alan had bribed Lacrosse to switch Phillip with Elizabeth's dead child.

17. *The mysterious Jennifer Richards turned out to be Amanda Wexler's mother, who had conceived Amanda during a tryst with her deceased sister's boyfriend. What was Jennifer's real name, what was her sister's name, how did the sister die, and who was the man in question?*

   a. Jane Marie Stafford; Janice; drowning; Alan Spaulding
   b. Janice Stafford; Jane Marie; suicide; Alan Spaulding
   c. Jennifer Wexler; Janet; drowning; Brandon Spaulding
   d. Jane Fletcher; Janice; run over by a car; Henry Chamberlain

18. *In what city had Ross Marler been engaged to Vanessa Chamberlain before they were reunited in Springfield?*

   a. New Orleans
   b. New York
   c. Detroit
   d. Chicago

19. *Whom or what did Quinton McCord conceal from his beloved Nola in his "third floor room"?*

   a. the charred remains of Nola's long-missing father, which Quinton was using for an archaeological experiment
   b. his birth certificate, which stated he was Sean Ryan, Henry Chamberlain's illegitimate son
   c. Mona Enright, his former love
   d. Helena Manzini, his mistress

20. *How many children does Bea Reardon have?*

   a. 4
   b. 6
   c. 7
   d. 11

THE SOAP OPERA *Digest* SCRAPBOOK

Guiding Light Crossword Puzzle

ACROSS

1. Dessert choice
4. Four-wheel drive Army car
8. Hair color
11. Word with flat or rubber
12. _____ Saunders = *DOOL*'s Marie Curtis
13. Actor Richard _____, star of *An Officer and a Gentleman*
14. Grant _____ = *GL*'s Phillip Spaulding
16. Rara _____ (special person); bird: Latin
17. _____ (21 Across) = *GL*'s Mike Bauer
18. _____ bien (very good: French)
19. Harley _____ = *GL*'s (31 Down) Sims
21. See 17 Across
23. Cut on an angle, like glass
24. _____ time, _____ where, _____ body
25. Grace Garland = *AMC*'s _____
26. A Gabor sister
29. Serving platters
32. Glass containers
33. Married
34. Ex-EON role, _____ Devereaux and others
35. Wingless insect
36. Fibbed
37. Author Anaïs _____

38. Rachel _____ = Audrey Hardy (*GH*)
39. Like a nitpicker; demanding
40. _____ Alicia = *FC*'s Melissa Cumson
41. Low numbers
42. Al Capp's "_____ Abner"
43. Robins, jays, etc.
45. Tom _____ = *GL*'s Floyd Parker
49. _____ Simon = one of the *GL* Bauers
50. Touch or sense
51. _____ Haddad = *OLTL*'s Cassie Callison

52. Lisa Brown = *GL*'s _____ Chamberlain
53. _____ = *GL*'s Maureen Reardon Bauer (full name)
56. Einar Perry Scott = *ATWT*'s _____ Anderson
57. Michael _____ = *GL*'s Jim Reardon
58. _____ Klaboe = *AW*'s Amanda Cory
59. Summer, in Paris
60. Nickname for _____ Pratt (*GL*'s Claire Ramsey), and others
61. *GL* Bauer played by 49 Across and others

DOWN

1. TV test show
2. _____ Dailey = *AW*'s Liz Matthews
3. Cartoon cry
4. Joanna Pettet = *KL*'s _____ Baines
5. Finishes; last parts
6. Opposite of WSW
7. *GL*'s Floyd and Katie
8. Kim Zimmer = *GL*'s _____ (full name)
9. TV star _____ Estrada
10. _____ Moines, Iowa
11. *AMC* role _____ Martin and others
12. _____ Gates = *GL*'s H. B. Lewis
13. Stare; look at
15. *DOOL*'s _____ Brock and others
20. Eggs: Latin
22. Directions; passages; courses
23. Charita Bauer = *GL*'s _____ Bauer (and others)
25. Weathercocks
27. Richard Van Vleet has two

28. Wesley _____ = Cabot Alden (*Loving*)
29. _____ Sloan = *GL*'s Lillian Raines
30. "Singin' in the _____"
31. See 19 Across
32. _____ McNichol = *GH*'s Josh
36. _____ to sleep (sing to sleep); break in the action
38. Warren Burton = *GL*'s Warren _____
39. Ballgame setting
41. Miner's find
42. Mortgages
44. *Play _____ It Lays:* Didion book (two words)
45. Wants
46. Word after egg or potato
47. Judi _____ = *GL*'s Beth Raines
48. "Peter Pan" dog
49. Rhyme maker
50. Iceberg
52. Opposite of SSW
54. Danielle Von Zerneck was _____ Swenson (*GH*)
55. "_____ to a Grecian Urn": Keats

THE **SOAP OPERA** *Digest* SCRAPBOOK

GUIDING LIGHT
Family Tree
1984

(father)
Bill Bauer — deceased

(mother)
Bert Bauer — works at hospital

(son)
Mike Bauer — lawyer

(son)
Ed Bauer — doctor

(son)
Rick Bauer — son of Ed and first wife Leslie; medical student; loves Mindy

Fletcher Reade — journalist

(daughter)
Hillary Bauer — nurse; had affairs with Kelly, Josh and Tony; involved with Jim

Claire Ramsey — doctor

(mother)
Lillian Raines — nurse

(daughter)
Beth Raines — college student; was engaged to Phillip; loves Lujack

Warren Andrews — President of Spaulding Foundation

(son)
Lujack — in love with Beth; works at Company

(uncle)
Ross Marler — President of Spaulding Enterprises; had affair with Trish

(daughter)
Trish Lewis — interior decorator; works for LTA; had affair with Ross

(son)
Billy Lewis — works for LTA Enterprises

(mother)
Alexandra Von Halkein — millionaire

(husband)
Phillip Spaulding — real son of Justin and late Jackie Marler; in love with Beth

(daughter)
Mindy Lewis Spaulding

108

GUIDING LIGHT

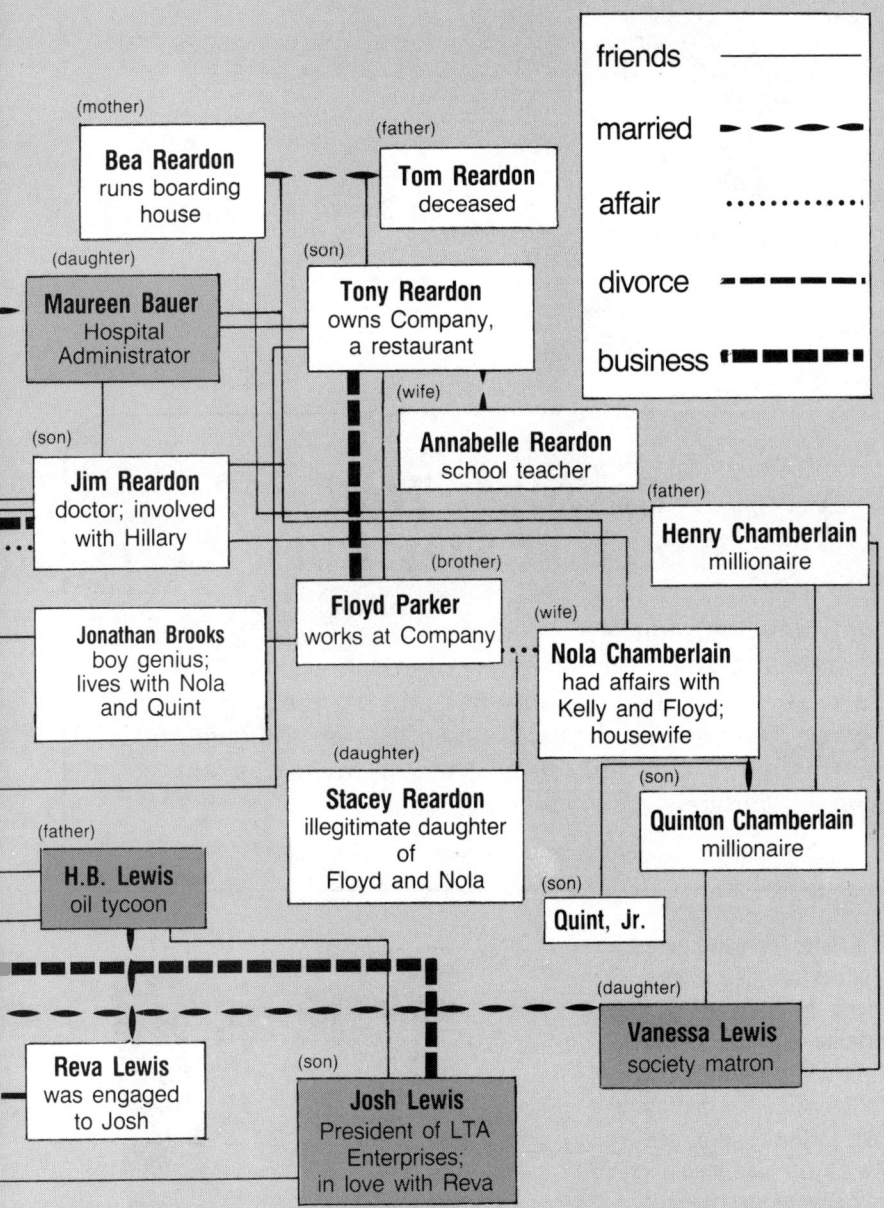

Don Stewart (Mike Bauer)

The Town That Wouldn't Stay Put

For many years on radio and television, *Guiding Light* was set in the Selby Flats section of Los Angeles. Then in the sixties, the locale suddenly became the medium-sized midwestern city of Springfield—even though the cast and sets remained intact, and the hospital in town was still known as Cedars!

Cute Krista Tesreau knocked the judges off their chairs when she won the Liberace Keyboard Entertainer Search, but as *Guiding Light*'s Mindy Lewis she's knocking Springfield on its ear. In the mold of her fellow Lewis clan members, Mindy always gets what and whom she wants. "Hell hath no fury" like Melinda Sue Lewis scorned!

Soaptrivia #8
WHERE'S HOME?

Match the show with its town setting and the correct setting *within* the setting (one of each per show). (This is a tricky one; not *all* the numbered and lower-case-lettered answers will be needed.)

A. *All My Children*
B. *Another World*
C. *As the World Turns*
D. *Days of Our Lives*
E. *General Hospital*
F. *Guiding Light*
G. *Loving*
H. *One Life to Live*
I. *Ryan's Hope*
J. *Search for Tomorrow*
K. *The Young and the Restless*

1. Llanview
2. Genoa City
3. New York City
4. Bay City
5. Salem
6. Denison
7. Pine Valley
8. Rosehill
9. Port Charles
10. Oakdale
11. Henderson
12. Madison
13. Springfield
14. Strathfield
15. Corinth

a. Alden University
b. The Press Box (restaurant)
c. Riverside Hospital
d. Jabot Cosmetics
e. The Riverboat (restaurant)
f. The Chateau (restaurant)
g. *The City Times* (newspaper)
h. The Versailles Room (restaurant)
i. Dream Faces (modeling agency)
j. Cedars Hospital
k. Tall Boy's (restaurant)
l. The Goal Post (restaurant)
m. The Coach House (restaurant)
n. *The Argus* (newspaper)
o. Shenanigans (restaurant)
p. Kelly's Diner

Augusta Dabney and Wesley Addy (Isabelle and Cabot Alden)

9
LOVING

Twenty Questions

1. The town of Corinth is located outside of what major city?

    a. Chicago
    b. Washington, DC
    c. Boston
    d. Cincinnati

2. Cabot Alden chairs the board at what institution of learning?

    a. Alden University
    b. Alden College
    c. Corinth University
    d. Forbes Technical College

3. What is the name of the Aldens' butler?

    a.   Heron   c.   Maynard

    b.   Chapin   d.   Soames

4. What does Billy Bristow do every night that infuriates his wife, Rita Mae?

    a.   plays piano rolls by the hour

    b.   dances to production numbers from *A Chorus Line,* which he plays on his stereo

    c.   practices with a new-wave rock band in which he is lead singer

    d.   runs college basketball plays on his videocassette machine in slow motion

Christopher Marcantel
(Curtis Alden)

LOVING

5. Who was the sleazy character who flirted with Lily Slater's oversexed alter ego during her bout with schizophrenia?

    a. Duke Schneider
    b. Dirk Snyder
    c. Kirk Michaels
    d. Kirk Snyder

6. What is Rose Donovan's maiden name?

    a. Moran
    b. O'Neill
    c. Riley
    d. Dooley

7. Who were the parents of Jim, Noreen, and Merrill Vochek?

    a. Carl and Lena
    b. Jack and Lena
    c. Vinny and Anna
    d. Jan and Freida

8. What tradition have the Donovan men observed for generations?

    a. breeding Irish setters
    b. buying three Christmas trees every holiday season
    c. taking off their shoes when Rose cleans the floor
    d. drinking Irish whiskey every Friday night

9. What is the name of the Irish pub that Mike and Douglas Donovan frequent?

    a. T. J. Moran's
    b. Dooley's
    c. Rooney's
    d. Ryan's

THE SOAP OPERA Digest SCRAPBOOK

10. *What was the name of the woman Cabot Alden impregnated years ago, who bore him an illegitimate daughter, Shana?*

    a. Kate Sloane
    b. Janet Sloane
    c. Lillian Sloane
    d. Lois Sloane

11. *Who were the two drug pushers who tried to pry Lorna away from Tony at the party where Mike made his famous drug bust?*

    a. Duke Rochelle and Chuck Ellis
    b. Dirk Snyder and Sam Moser
    c. Duke Snyder and Chuck Moser
    d. Chuck Rochelle and Clem Moser

12. *What is the name of the dizzy blonde waitress Curtis Alden occasionally dates, and where does she work?*

    a. Connie O'Neill; The Hideaway
    b. Penny O'Rourke; The Hideaway
    c. Peggy O'Shea; Dooley's
    d. Molly McGuire; The Elms

13. *At which two television stations did Merrill Vochek appear as a newscaster, and which of the two did Cabot Alden own?*

    a. WCRN, WMON; WCRN
    b. WCN, WCR; WCN
    c. WCOR, WPA; WCOR
    d. WCN, WCR; WCR

14. *What are Jack Forbes's two talents, which have made him a "big man on campus"?*

    a. football and basketball
    b. baseball and basketball

Loving's sympathetic character of Noreen Vochek Donovan (Marilyn McIntyre) may be the sister of a Catholic priest, but even she couldn't hack a disintegrating 10-year marriage to an embittered Viet Nam vet who refused to deal with his complex psychological problems.

    c.   classical piano playing and PA announcing

    d.   None; he's the class nerd

15.   Who was the first person Jack consulted when he discovered Garth Slater was sexually abusing his daughter, Lily?

    a.   Dr. Ron Turner

    b.   Lt. Art Hindman

    c.   Sgt. Mike Donovan

    d.   Father Jim Vochek

16.   What is the name of the department store that Shana Sloane helped to revamp?

    a.   Tyrell's   c.   Pendleton's

    b.   Alderman's   d.   Burnell's

17.   Who murdered Garth Slater?

    a.   Johnny Forbes   c.   Lily Slater

    b.   June Slater   d.   Dirk Rochelle

18. Who was the dead army buddy who appeared in Mike Donovan's hallucinations?

    a. Gage Robinson

    b. Roosevelt Gage

    c. Charlie Gage

    d. Charlie Robertson

19. Which one of these women was Curtis Alden's first sexual conquest after the show premiered?

    a. Lily Slater

    b. Stacey Donovan

    c. Lorna Forbes

    d. Rita Mae Bristow

20. What is the line of work of Rose Donovan's husband, Patrick?

    a. He drives a truck.

    b. He's head of security for Alden University.

    c. He's a retired carpenter.

    d. None; he's an alcoholic bum the family is ashamed of.

LOVING

Loving Word Search

Soap-related words are hidden in this maze of letters. They read forward, backward, up, down, or diagonally, always in a straight line. Circle the letters as you find them. Letters may be used more than once. The remaining letters will (in order) spell a hidden message. To start, we have indicated the first word in bold type. Enjoy!

A	R	F	T	N	S	E	B	R	O	F	K	C	A	J
L	A	A	O	E	N	A	E	K	I	R	E	T	A	S
C	P	T	N	R	T	U	R	N	E	R	L	M	K	J
O	E	H	Y	R	A	N	E	D	L	A	E	N	E	J
H	E	E	P	A	Y	E	C	A	T	S	A	N	U	A
O	N	R	E	W	L	O	V	T	K	B	N	N	L	M
L	A	J	R	I	O	N	S	I	U	I	E	I	L	A
I	O	I	E	G	R	E	B	E	F	S	L	L	N	R
S	L	M	L	E	C	E	N	E	L	Y	I	Y	A	D
M	S	Y	L	N	R	O	R	A	V	R	L	L	R	O
U	A	D	I	D	N	A	T	E	R	I	R	L	E	H
R	N	D	Y	N	S	E	R	E	R	M	I	I	T	C
D	A	A	A	H	R	I	M	A	N	U	T	B	E	Y
E	H	H	E	E	T	O	M	L	I	G	O	N	V	S
R	S	U	S	A	N	W	O	R	B	R	E	T	E	P

119

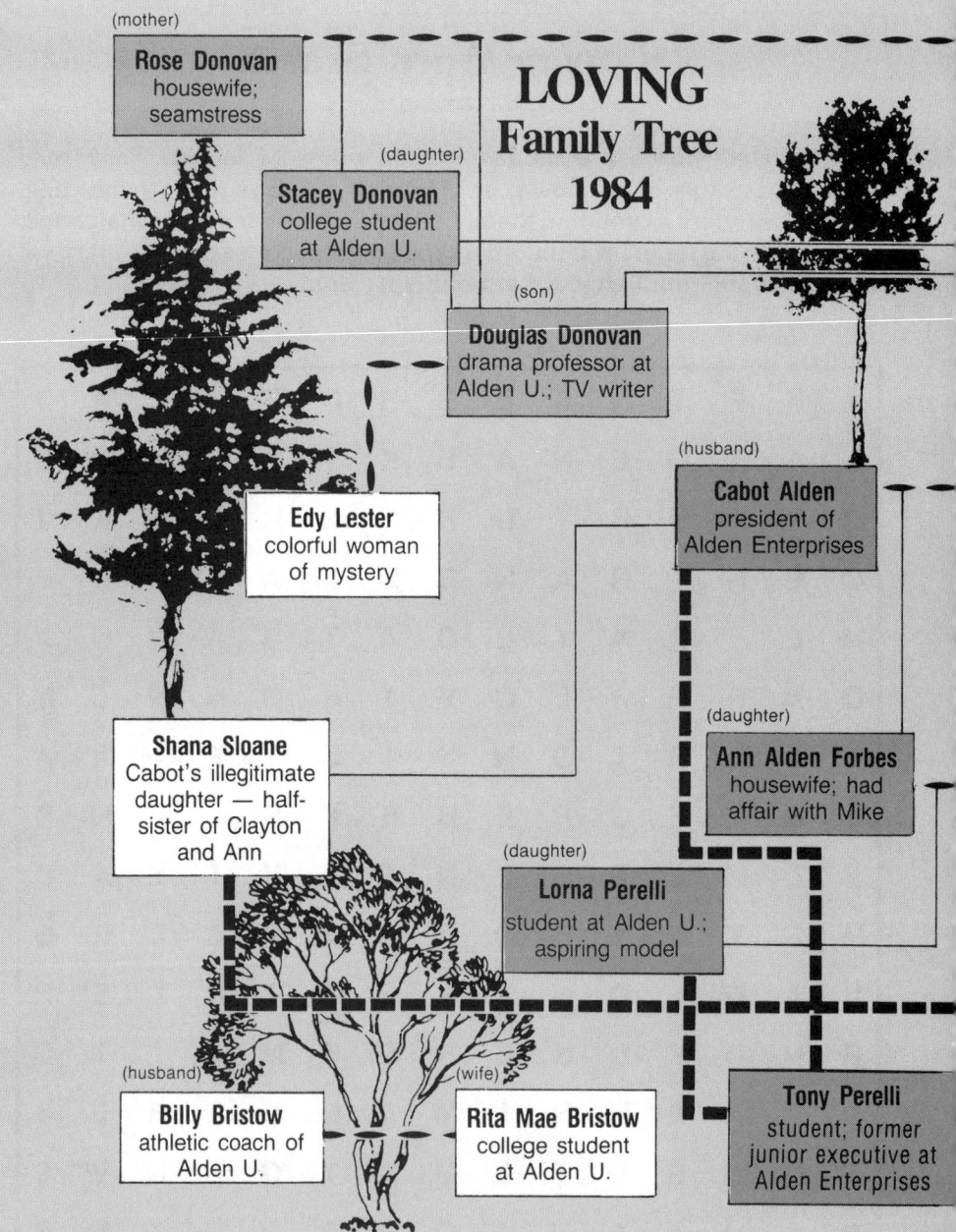

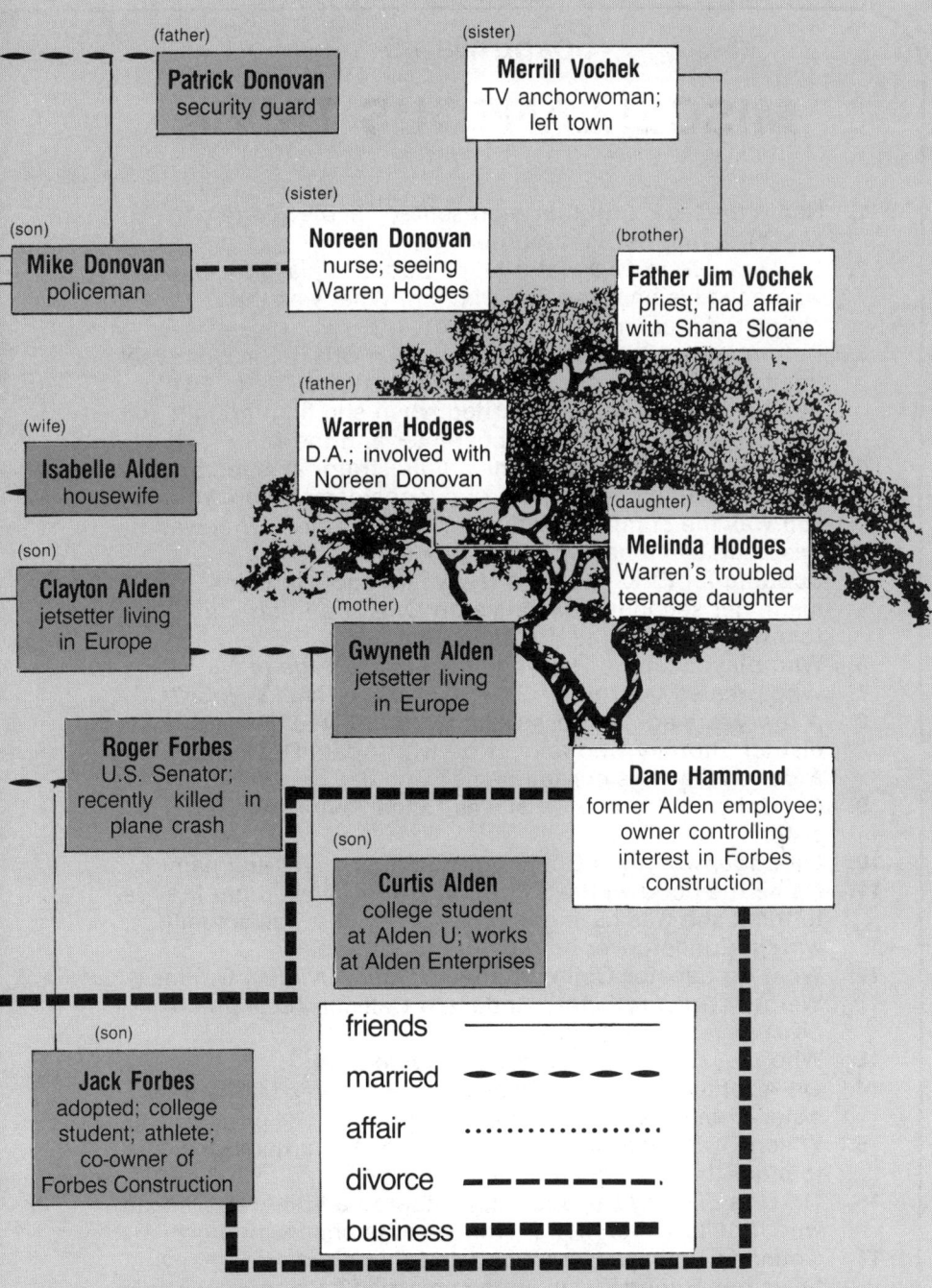

THE SOAP OPERA *Digest* SCRAPBOOK

Soaptrivia #9
MISCELLANEOUS TRIVIA

1. Name the legal firm that represented Nicole (*Edge of Night*) during her first murder trial.
2. On *One Life to Live,* actor Mark Goddard played a villain who gave his name as Ted Clayton. What was the character's real name?
3. Before appearing as mob kingpin Dan Briskin on *Somerset,* this talented actor stirred things up on *One Life to Live* as the man Viki Buchanan married when she first thought Joe Riley was dead. Name the character and the actor.
4. Actor Robert Milli played the administrator at Cedars Hospital (*Guiding Light*), a kind, considerate man whose son was the complete antithesis of the father. What was this character's name?
5. Subbing for Erika Slezak a few years ago, Christine Jones made her second appearance on *One Life to Live*. In what role was she cast the first time?
6. Who played Margo Huntington Dorn on *Edge of Night*?
7. Who created the role of Dr. Pat Ryan on *Ryan's Hope*?
8. A few years ago, actress Dixie Carter played an assistant district attorney who fell in love with Adam Drake (*Edge of Night*). What was her full name?
9. On *General Hospital,* what was Diana Taylor's younger sister's name?
10. On *Edge,* what was Cookie Christopher's real first name?
11. Name the hood with whom Nancy Karr allowed her friends to think she was having an affair when she was actually working undercover on a story for the paper.
12. What do Senator Colin Whitney (*Edge of Night*), Dr. Joe Werner (*Guiding Light*), and Herb Callison (*One Life to Live*) have in common?
13. Who played Dr. Tim Ryan on *Guiding Light*?
14. On *Another World,* what was the name of Liz Matthews's sister-in-law? Also, who played her?
15. Which CBS soap was the first to have a character give birth to more than two children at a time?
16. On *One Life to Live,* Joe Riley fathered a little girl, Meagan, who didn't live very long. Who was the child's mother?
17. Counting both *Another World* and *Somerset,* how many times has Robert Delaney been married? Name his wives in chronological order.
18. Who played ballerina Martine Duval on *The Edge of Night*?

19. Before his return to *The Edge of Night* as the real Gunther Wagner, David Froman played Gunther's twin, who decided to masquerade as his brother. Name the first brother, the one killed by Jefferson Brown.
20. Name the bartender on *Ryan's Hope,* who is practically a member of the family.
21. When Genie Francis began playing *GH's*'s Laura Faulkner (later Spencer), how was her name listed in the credits?
22. On *Days of Our Lives,* what is Don Craig's secret hobby?
23. Who played Phillip Wainwright on *AW*? Name the spoiled heiress who paid him to break up her father's marriage.
24. Who played Marianne Randolph's first boyfriend, Chris, on *AW,* then went on to play an art teacher on *GL*?
25. Annie and Dee are nicknames for the Stewart sisters on *As the World Turns.* What are their full names?
26. How many times has *AMC*'s Tara Martin been legally married? Name her husbands in chronological order.
27. Before starring on *Capitol,* Constance Towers appeared on another CBS soap. Which one was it; whom did she play?
28. Who succeeded James Houghton in the role of *The Young & the Restless*'s Greg Foster?
29. What was the illness from which Brock Reynolds (*Y&R*) fought to save his mother? Name the mother.
30. How many actors have played *All My Children*'s Jeff Martin? Name them, as well as his three wives—both in chronological order.
31. What kind of flower did the mysterious Helena Cassadine pin in Luke Spencer's lapel before his wedding (*GH*)?
32. What raven-haired superstar appeared as Helena Cassadine on *General Hospital*?
33. What did Helena Cassadine (*General Hospital*) have her henchman steal from Luke and Laura in order to put her curse on them?
34. Who created the role of Russ Matthews on *Another World*?
35. What did *All My Children*'s Nick Davis, Jason Maxwell, and Brandon Kingsley have in common?
36. What was the hometown of Blaine and Larry Ewing before they moved to Bay City (*Another World*)?
37. Angie and Joey Perrini's mother (*Another World*) often watched Jamie Frame when he was growing up; later, his much younger aunt baby-sat as well. Name Jamie's aunt and give Mrs. Perrini's first name.
38. What is the last name of the district attorney on *GH*?
39. How many actresses have appeared on *Ryan's Hope* as Amanda Kirkland? Name them.
40. Who played Felicia Lamont on *Love of Life*? Also, name her famous director-husband.

Erika Slezak (Viki Buchanan)

10
ONE LIFE TO LIVE

Twenty Questions

1. Viki Buchanan's deceased sister was Dan Wolek's mother. What was her name?

    a. Joanne
    b. Eleanor
    c. Hester
    d. Meredith

2. What unseen tyrant heads the city room at the Banner newspaper?

    a. Briggs
    b. Riggs
    c. Griggs
    d. Biggs

3. Where did Cathy Craig obtain drug rehabilitation?

    a. Her father, Dr. Jim Craig, did it all himself.
    b. Phoenix House
    c. Chapin House
    d. Odyssey House

THE SOAP OPERA Digest SCRAPBOOK

4. Eileen, the devout Irish Catholic sister of the late Joe Riley, was married to what now-deceased Jewish lawyer?

    a. Jake Spiegel
    b. Irv Segal
    c. Dave Siegel
    d. Bernie Siegel

5. Who was Victor Lord's first wife, and which was the only one of his three children conceived by him and his wife?

    a. Eugenia; Joanne
    b. Dorothy; Tony
    c. Eleanor; Viki
    d. Eugenia; Meredith

6. Who was Dorian's first lover when she came to Llanview?

    a. Mark Toland
    b. Matt McAllister
    c. John Douglas
    d. Ramsey Overton

7. Years ago the Woleks, the Rileys, and the Grays lived in what downtrodden area?

    a. South Philadelphia
    b. South Boston
    c. Sea City
    d. Watts

8. Who was Will Vernon's wife, and how did she die?

    a. Naomi; drowned in a river
    b. Pamela; killed in a car accident
    c. Pamela; suicide
    d. Naomi; suicide

9. Who were Carla Gray's love interests before her first marriage to Ed Hall?

    a. Price Trainor, Jack Scott
    b. Bert Skelly, Jack Scott
    c. Price Trainor, Bert Skelly
    d. Josh West, Jack Scott

ONE LIFE TO LIVE

10. What was the name of Pat Ashley's murderous twin?

    a. Maggie
    b. Helena
    c. Gretel
    d. Lana

11. Which of these men never shared a bed with Karen Wolek?

    a. Talbot Huddleston
    b. Ivan Kipling
    c. Marco Dane
    d. Dan Wolek

12. What was Ivan Kipling's offbeat sexual fetish?

    a. black pantyhose
    b. black negligées
    c. black spiked-heel shoes
    d. army boots

13. For whom did Anna Wolek carry a torch when she married Jim Craig?

    a. Victor Lord
    b. Walter Witherspoon
    c. Joe Riley
    d. Senator Charlton

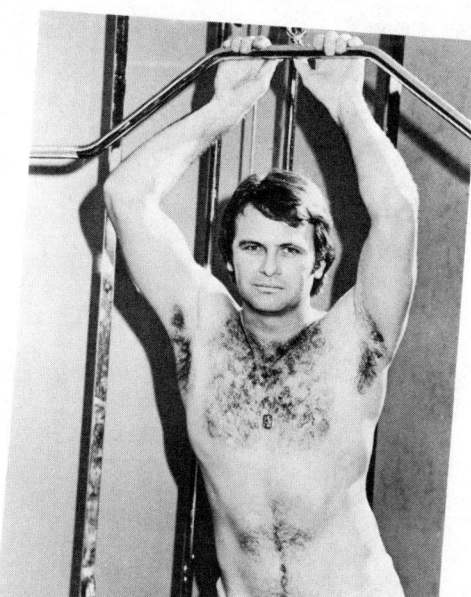

Robert S. Woods (Bo Buchanan)

Photo by Kacey Associates Inc.

14. Which one of these characters was never a member of the Llanview Hospital board?

    a. Dennis O'Reardon
    b. Asa Buchanan
    c. Col. William Hutchinson
    d. Dorian Callison

15. Whom did Olympia Buchanan falsely name as Bo's natural father?

    a. Yancy Ralston
    b. Asa Buchanan
    c. Chuck Wilson
    d. Col. William Hutchinson

16. What was the name of Tina Clayton's mother, and what was her connection to Viki?

    a. Irene Clayton; college roommate
    b. Irene Clayton; half-sister
    c. Eugenia Clayton; college roommate
    d. Rachel Clayton; total stranger

17. What was the hobby of Melinda Cramer, Dorian's fragile sister?

    a. stamp collecting
    b. classical piano playing
    c. country-western singing
    d. rock guitar playing

18. Which concern is not in Dorian Callison's sphere of control?

    a. *The Banner*
    b. Llanview Hospital

ONE LIFE TO LIVE

"The Moving Finger... Having Writ, Moves On...."

Long before he was headwriter of *One Life to Live* Sam Hall penned CBS's now-defunct *The Brighter Day* at the peak of its popularity. Unfortunately, the show's iron-fisted creator, the legendary Irna Phillips (deceased), complained that Sam's stories moved too fast and wormed her way back into the headwriting position. Sam was so incensed by his dismissal that he made sure Irna inherited a story mess that would take a year to clean up, including the defrocking of the minister who was the show's main character! What happened? The show took such a nose dive after Sam left that it never recovered. CBS dropped the show a few years later.

  c. WVLE-TV
  d. Llanview West western-style bar

19. Where did Karen and Marco hide when they were on the run, and from what were they running?

  a. a carnival; counterfeiters
  b. a carnival; a prostitution ring
  c. a little theater company; a Communist organization
  d. a carnival; Asa Buchanan

20. In the San Carlos fortune caper, what did Cristofori ultimately turn out to be?

  a. a pizzeria   c. a piano
  b. a hit man   d. a dachshund with a brain implant

One Life to Live Crossword Puzzle

ACROSS

1. *The Thin Man* dog
5. Flippered water animal
9. Sandra of films
12. With 9 Down, first name of Snyder who plays *OLTL*'s 30 Down O'Neill
13. _____ VandenBosch = *ATWT*'s Frannie Hughes
14. Sound receiver
15. Ellen Holly = *OLTL*'s Carla _____
16. Actress Stevens; spring month
17. _____ Haddad = *OLTL*'s Cassie Callison
18. Snake that bit Cleopatra
19. Tim _____ = *OLTL*'s Simon Warfield
21. _____ Caudell = ex-Woody King (*DOOL*) and others
23. Israeli dance
24. Street in almost every town
26. Actress Gray (*Buck Rogers*) and others
28. Dorian Lopinto = *OLTL*'s _____ Vernon
32. Depend (with "on")
33. Phylicia Ayers _____ = *OLTL*'s Courtney Wright
34. Holbrook or Linden
35. "The _____ That I Marry": Rodgers and Hammerstein
36. Ways to weight loss
37. Opposite of departures: *Abbr.*
38. Cassius Clay, _____ Muhammad Ali

39. Philip _____ = *OLTL*'s Mr. Buchanan
40. "_____ the Rainbow"
41. Steven Culp = *OLTL*'s _____ (full name)
43. Winter weather
44. Made angry
45. TV camera workers
46. Jeremy _____ = *OLTL*'s Chuck Wilson
49. "The _____ on the Hill": Beatles hit
50. Mom's mate
53. Jimmy's late mother, for short

54. _____ Edmonds = *AMC*'s Langley Wallingford
57. Mirror reflection
59. Janet Grey = ex-*GL*'s _____ McFarren
60. Michael Storm = *OLTL*'s _____ Wolek
61. Jeff _____ = *OLTL*'s Gary (39 Down)
62. Santa's mo.
63. Gossip column note
64. Slippery fish

DOWN

1. Circle segments
2. Feast for pigs
3. Asian holiday
4. Gerald _____ = *OLTL*'s Marco Dane
5. Fall mo.
6. Make a mistake
7. Jackie's last hubby
8. _____ Hayman = *OLTL*'s Sadie Gray
9. See 12 Across (middle name)
10. Roof overhang
11. Geological time periods
12. Mr. Buchanan of 39 Across
13. Dr. Joe's absent daughter (*AMC*)
20. _____ gratia artis: M-G-M's motto
22. _____ Flood = *EON*'s Nancy Karr
23. Roger _____ = *OLTL*'s 48 Down Lowndes
24. Like a brewery product
25. Family name on *The Secret Storm*
26. _____ Slezak = *OLTL*'s Viki Riley Buchanan
27. Showed again on TV
28. Smooth and glossy

29. Pitched; tossed
30. Mr. O'Neill of 12 Across and 9 Down
31. *OLTL*'s _____ Freeman and others
33. Broadcast; put on TV or radio
35. Mild oath; wander about
36. Roy Rogers's wife, _____ Evans
37. Make _____ (promise; two words); swear
39. See 61 Across
40. Part of *OLTL* (two words)
42. Cleverness; glib talker
43. Sign for a sold-out show: Abbr.
45. Comfy (variant)
46. Santa's vehicle
47. Another part of *OLTL*
48. See 23 Down
49. Company; unmoving; set
50. Arlene _____ = *OLTL*'s Lucinda Schenk
51. Grows old
52. Tunisian pasha
55. Cereal in a horse's bag
56. Stage actress Mary _____
58. Pamela Blair = *Loving*'s Rita _____ Bristow

THE SOAP OPERA *Digest* SCRAPBOOK

ONE LIFE TO LIVE
Family Tree 1984

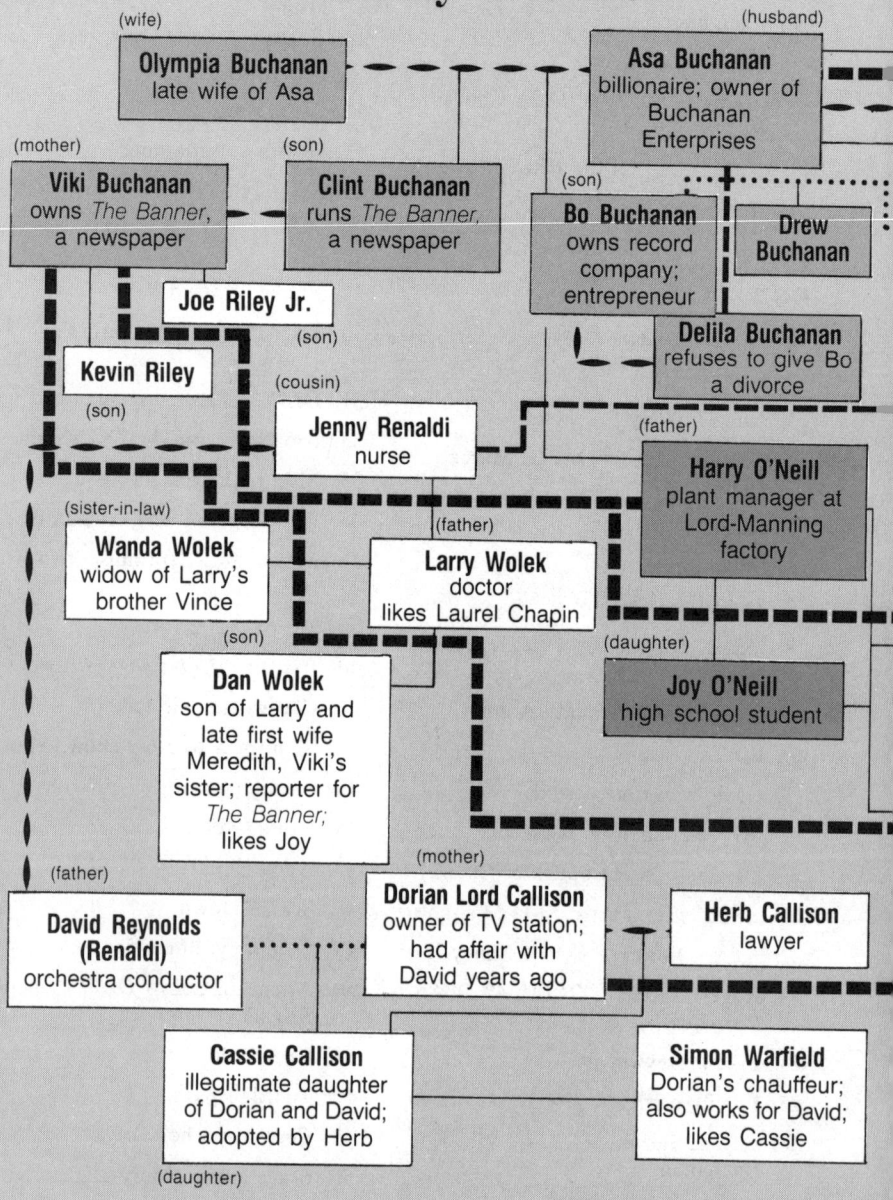

ONE LIFE TO LIVE

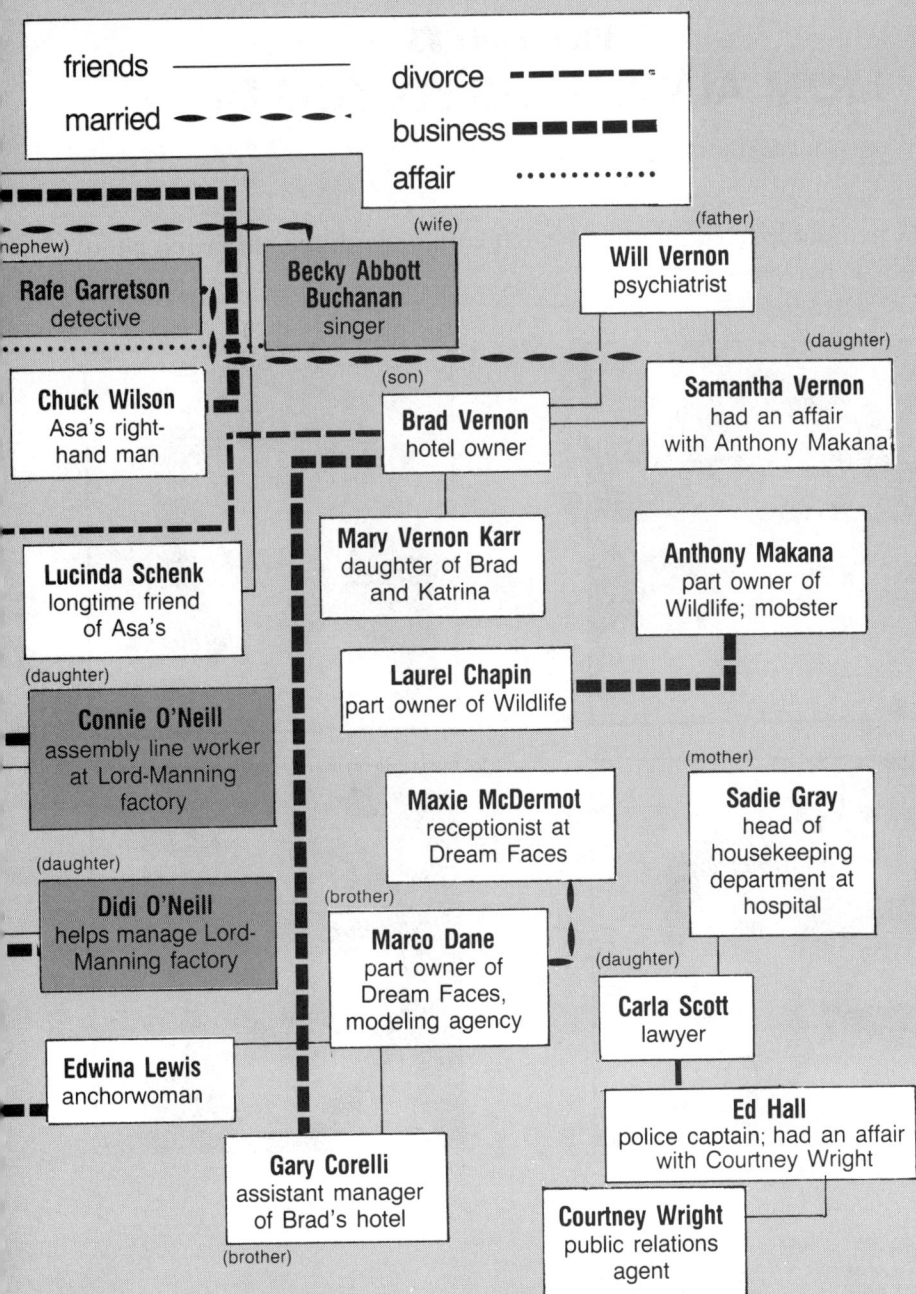

THE **SOAP OPERA** *Digest* SCRAPBOOK

Photoquiz #3
MOM ALWAYS LIKED YOU BEST

Match the lettered photo in the left column with the numbered photo of his or her on-screen sibling.

A

1

B

2

PHOTOQUIZ

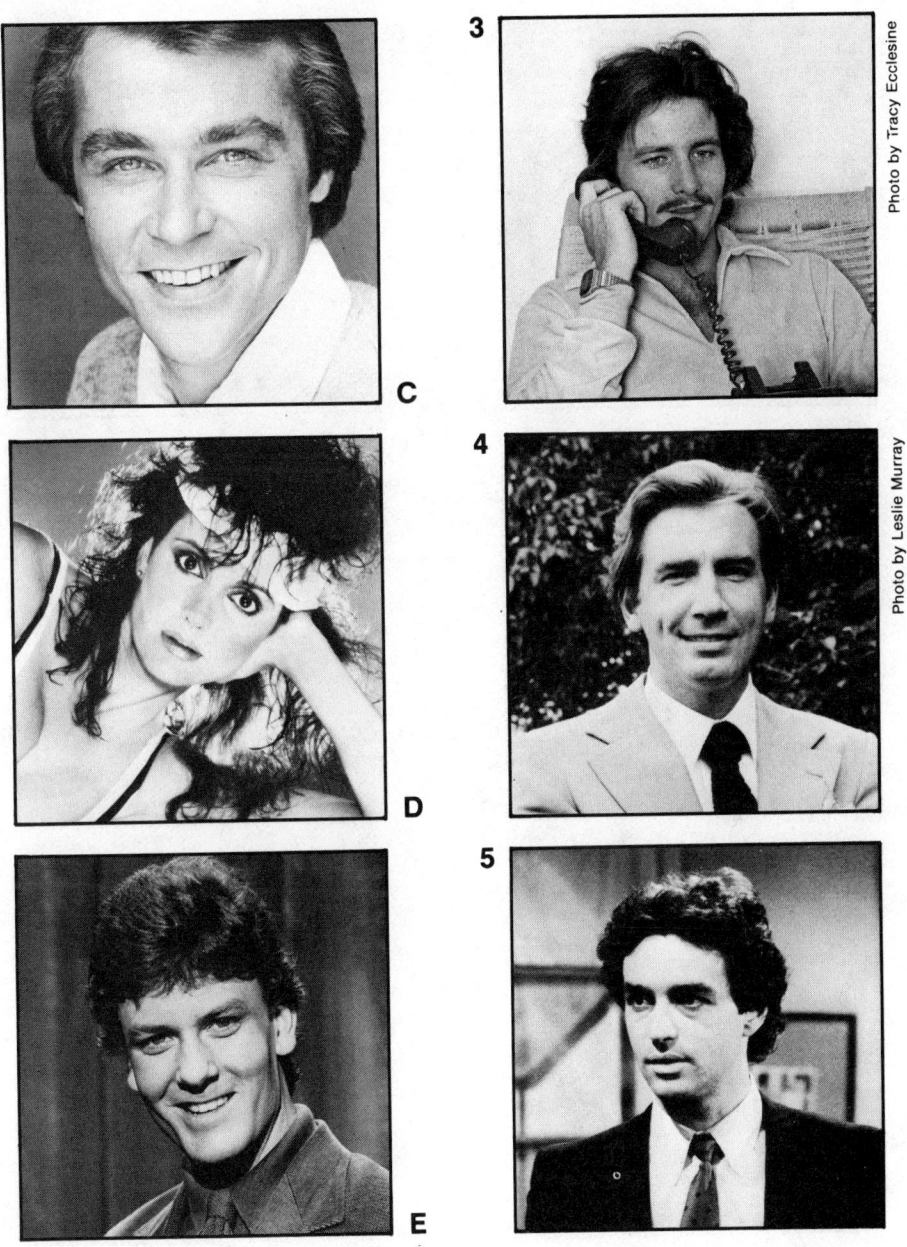

THE SOAP OPERA *Digest* SCRAPBOOK

F

G

H

Photo by Leslie Murray

PHOTOQUIZ

Photo by Ed Geller

Soaptrivia # 10
TRUE OR FALSE?

1. Christina Pickles of NBC's *St. Elsewhere* created the *Another World* role now played by Maeve McGuire.
2. Elena dePoulignac (*Another World*) once had an affair with Dennis Carrington.
3. Marie Masters appeared on *One Life to Live* as lawyer Helen Beaumont.
4. Stacey Winthrop (*Another World*) is Cass's ex-wife.
5. During their pursuit of Stefano DiMera (*Days of Our Lives*) Abe remained on active duty while Roman went undercover as a drug smuggler who called himself "Mr. Snow."
6. Karen and Jenny Wolek (*One Life to Live*) grew up in a New York brownstone.
7. Georgina Whitman (*One Life to Live*) was working on a method to devise an alternative energy source using a mineral called *solarimite*.
8. Alan Gifford once played the deranged Keith Whitney on *The Edge of Night*.
9. Little Bobby Warner's mother (*All My Children*) was troublemaking nurse Sybil Thorne.
10. Edward Winter played *Another World*'s Harry Shea.

SOAPTRIVIA

11. Richard Thomas once appeared on *As the World Turns*.
12. Christopher George played the young Mike Bauer on *Guiding Light*.
13. Actresses Kathryn Hays, Maeve McGuire, and Mary Page Keller have all played amnesia victims.
14. Child actor Trip Randall played *Love of Life*'s Johnny Prentiss.
15. Delia Coleridge (*Ryan's Hope*) once pushed her first husband down a flight of stairs, crippling him temporarily.
16. The maid in the DiMera house (*Days of Our Lives*) is named Amanda.
17. Quint McCord (*Guiding Light*) is really Amanda Wexler's half-brother.
18. Sally Frame's ex-husband is Dennis Carrington (*Another World*).
19. Eve McFarren (*Guiding Light*) is the sister of Helena Manzini.
20. Alison Bancroft (*The Young and the Restless*) was ecstatic over her son's marriage to Nikki Reed.

Nancy Addison Altman (Jillian Ryan).

11 RYAN'S HOPE

Twenty Questions

1. Where did Jack Fenelli work before his days as a reporter?

    a. in a foundry

    b. in a Hell's Kitchen saloon

    c. on the docks

    d. in a sausage factory

2. What is the medical specialty of Seneca Beaulac and Roger Coleridge?

    a. neurology

    b. cardiac surgery

    c. proctology

    d. gynecology

3. How did Seneca meet Jillian Coleridge?

    a. She had a flat tire, which he happened along to fix.

    b. She was a patient in Riverside Hospital.

    c. She defended him for his mercykilling of his wife, Nell.

    d. She defended him for malpractice.

4. Which one of these men never married Delia Reid?

    a. Barry Ryan   c. Pat Ryan

    b. Frank Ryan   d. Roger Coleridge

5. Where did Mary and Jack Fenelli set up residence?

    a. Riverside Drive

    b. West End Avenue

    c. Avenue B

    d. Weehawken Street

6. Jack was stoical after Mary's death until Maeve sang a song that triggered enough memories for Jack to break into tears. What was the song?

    a. " 'Twas Only an Irishman's Dream"

    b. "Danny Boy"

    c. "That's an Irish Lullaby"

    d. "Macnamara's Band"

7. Who is chief of staff at Riverside Hospital?

    a. Seneca Beaulac

    b. Roger Coleridge

    c. Marshall Westheimer

    d. Ruth Westheimer

8. Where did Maeve and Johnny Ryan meet?

    a. Ireland
    b. Riverside Church
    c. Chelsea
    d. Brooklyn

9. Siobhan Ryan returned home after a long absence with a dog she presented to her delighted father, Johnny. What were the breed and name of the dog?

    a. Irish setter; Red
    b. Irish setter; Casey
    c. Irish wolfhound; Finn McCool
    d. Irish wolfhound; Kevin

10. Who was Jack's lifelong father figure and confidant?

    a. Jumbo Marino
    b. Tiso Novotny
    c. Johnny Ryan
    d. Dr. Ed Coleridge

11. What was the name of the gorilla who did his King Kong/Fay Wray number with Delia?

    a. Prince Valiant
    b. Prince Albert
    c. Prince Charles
    d. Prince

12. Rose Melina, Jack's former flame, had a daughter who had become the adopted granddaughter of syndicate boss Alexei Vartova. What was the girl's name?

a. Mariarosa
b. Amelia
c. Donna
d. Patricia

13. E. J. Ryan infiltrated the cast of a popular soap opera to get a story. Which is the correct combination of title, star, and headwriting team for the fictional serial?

    a. "Our Brighter Years"; Barbara Wilding; Ira and Margaret Phillips
    b. "Yelen Falls"; Viveca Wilding; Dina and Douglas Dobson
    c. "When Push Comes to Shove"; Barbara Wyle; Peter and Penny Pollock
    d. "The Proud and the Passionate"; Barbara Wilde; Hannah and Harry Harcourt

14. What was the name of the legendary deceased Egyptian figure who was the subject of a mystery involving Faith Coleridge and Aristotle Benedict-White?

    a. Maritkera
    b. Meritkera
    c. Amarika
    d. Kasimira

15. Who was the man that Rae Woodard and Kimberly Harris were accused of murdering, and who ultimately turned out to be the killer?

    a. Michael Pavel; Alexei Vartova
    b. Michael Pavel; Sal Brooks
    c. Bill Woodard; Wes Leonard
    d. Wes Leonard; Sal Brooks

Malcolm Groome (Dr. Patrick Ryan).

16. Where do Cathleen and Art Thompson, Frank Ryan's sister and brother-in-law, reside?

    a. Elmira, New York

    b. Valley Stream, New York

    c. Pittsburgh, Pennsylvania

    d. Hallandale, Florida

17. Who was the doomed rock star who had a brief encounter with Jillian?

    a. Peter Paul Post   c. Ken George Jones

    b. Kenny Joe Jones   d. Paul George Post

18. Who was the devout Jewish man whose daughter was romantically involved with Pat Ryan?

   a. Dave Feldman
   b. George Bloom
   c. Dave Maskin
   d. Sam Berlin

19. What is the name of Hollis Kirkland's power-wielding wife?

   a. Kitsy
   b. Catsy
   c. Fritzi
   d. Mitzi

20. What ultimately happened to Kimberly Harris Beaulac?

   a. She was institutionalized.
   b. She left town with her amorous manager.
   c. She left town with Hollis Kirkland, her long-lost father.
   d. She left town with Hollis Kirkland, her new husband.

Ryan's Hope Word Search

Soap-related words are hidden in this maze of letters. They read forward, backward, up, down, or diagonally, always in a straight line. Circle the letters as you find them. Letters may be used more than once. The remaining letters will (in order) spell a hidden message. To start, we have indicated the first word in bold type. Enjoy!

```
N A H B O I S T H M A E V E K
A D N A L K R I K S J D X E E
N O V O T N Y C E O E P S G N
C F L A S H A M E H L E E D N
Y N N H O J L N A O D N N I Y
A H L B U O O V S N I N E R T
D I A B H V E I A L P A C E I
D N U P A N O L E E R Y A L C
I D R K R N R U A I U R B O K
S M E I R E Q G N G D K E C R
O A N E Z C G A T G E N A R O
N N E T A P P N R A N A U E Y
L R I J E A D V A M C R L G W
G W E J A I L L E N E F A O E
S N T U R A I F A M T E C R N
```

147

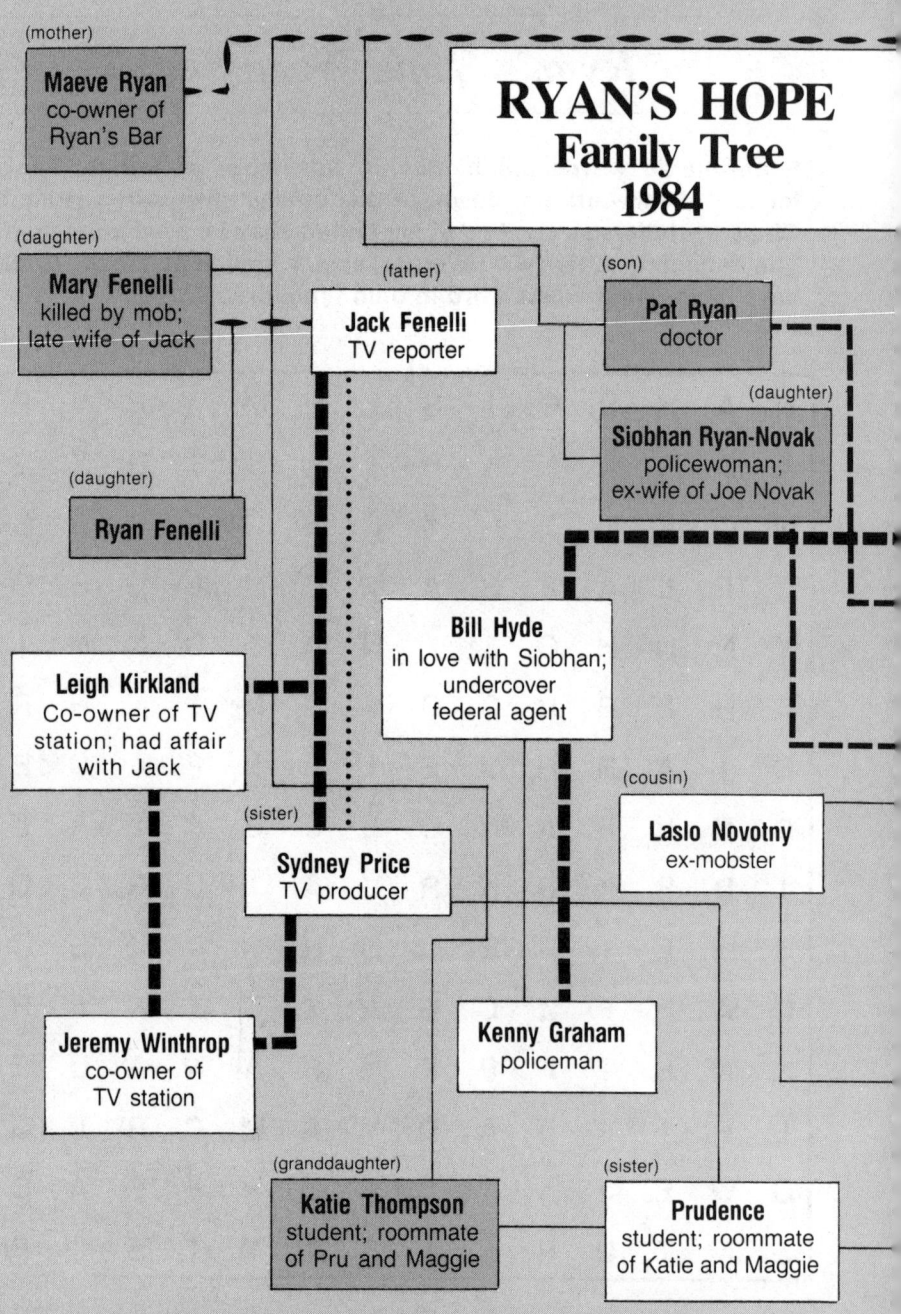

RYAN'S HOPE

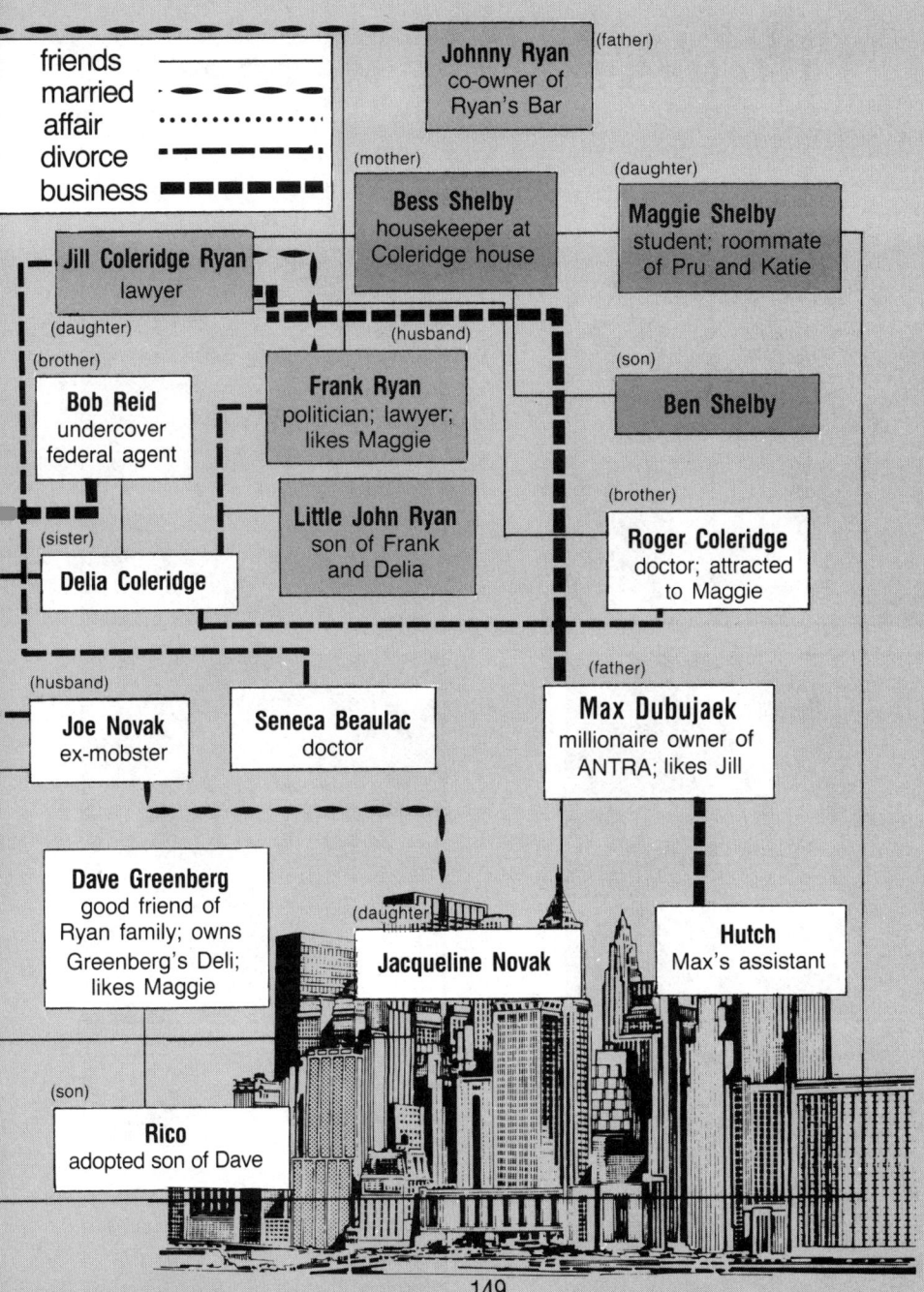

THE **SOAP OPERA** *Digest* SCRAPBOOK

Photoquiz #4
THANKS FOR THE MEMORY

In the following cases, what the writers hath joined, the writers also put asunder—either by death or by divorce. Match each person in the left column with his or her former partner in the right column.

Soaptrivia # 11
FROM WHENCE THEY CAME, PART II

Match the current popular soap actress with the correct list of her past soap roles.

A. Jacqueline Courtney (Alice Matthews, *Another World*)
B. Leslie Charleson (Dr. Monica Quartermaine, *General Hospital*)
C. Lee Lawson (Bea Reardon, *Guiding Light*)
D. Robin Strasser (Dorian Callison, *One Life to Live*)
E. Mary Fickett (Ruth Martin, *All My Children*)
F. Augusta Dabney (Isabelle Alden, *Loving*)
G. Susan Brown (Dr. Gail Baldwin, *General Hospital*)
H. Elizabeth Lawrence (Myra Murdoch, *All My Children*)
I. Susan Keith (Shana Sloane, *Loving*)
J. Sally Gracie (Ina Hopkins, *One Life to Live*)
K. Ruth Warrick (Phoebe Wallingford, *All My Children*)
L. Kim Zimmer (Reva Lewis, *Guiding Light*)
M. Marilyn McIntyre (Noreen Donovan, *Loving*)
N. Ann Flood (Nancy Karr, *Edge of Night*)
O. Kay Campbell (Kate Martin, *All My Children*)
P. Victoria Wyndham (Rachel Cory, *Another World*)
Q. Tina Sloan (Lillian Raines, *Guiding Light*)
R. Teri Keane (Rose Donovan, *Loving*)
S. Gillian Spencer (Daisy Cortlandt, *All My Children*)
T. Constance Ford (Ada Hobson, *Another World*)

1. Meg Blaine, *As the World Turns*; Martha Marceau, *Edge of Night*; Naomi Vernon, *One Life to Live*
2. Janet Johnson, *Guiding Light*; Edith Hughes Frye, *As the World Turns*
3. Sally Smith, *Edge of Night*; Liz Thorpe, *The Nurses*; Dr. Katherine Lovell, *Edge of Night*

4. Liz Fraser Allen, *From These Roots*
5. Liz Fraser Allen, *From These Roots*; Ann Reynolds, *The Young Marrieds*; Martha Ferguson, *Bright Promise*; Constance Carson, *Return to Peyton Place;* Fran Whittaker, *The Young and the Restless*
6. Rose Peterson, *Search for Tomorrow*; Lynn Sherwood, *Woman with a Past*; Eve Morris, *Edge of Night*
7. Alice Whipple, *As the World Turns*; Iris Donnelly Garrison, *Love Is a Many Splendored Thing*
8. Samantha Vernon, *One Life to Live*; Cecile dePoulignac, *Another World*
9. Lyn Wilkins Warren, *Edge of Night*; Robin Fletcher, *Guiding Light*; Victoria Lord, *One Life to Live*; Jennifer Hughes, *As the World Turns*
10. Viola Smith, *Edge of Night*; Anne Lee, *Our Five Daughters*; Pat Ashley, *One Life to Live*
11. Kate Thornton Cannell, *Somerset*; Patti Whiting, *Search for Tomorrow*
12. Rachel Davis, *Another World*; Dr. Christina Karras, *All My Children*
13. Barbara Sterling Latimer, *Love of Life*; Wanda Wolek, *One Life to Live*
14. Helene Benedict, *Guiding Light*; Rose Pollock, *Edge of Night*
15. Tracey Malone, *Young Doctor Malone*; Laura Baxter, *Another World*; Anne Holmes, *As the World Turns*; Peg Hale, *Love Is a Many Splendored Thing*; Betty Kahlman Barry, *A World Apart*; Carolyn Chandler Baldwin, *General Hospital*; Helena Ashley, *One Life to Live*; Theodora van Alen, *The Doctors*
16. Francie Brent, *The Road of Life*; Constance Johnson, *Edge of Night*; Vera Turek, *Edge of Night*; Betty Kahlman Barry, *A World Apart*; Margaret Higgins, *Somerset*; Virginia Dancy, *The Doctors*
17. Dr. Carolyn Hanley, *Search for Tomorrow*; Astrid Collins, *One Life to Live*; Sydney Galloway, *Ryan's Hope*
18. Charlotte Waring, *Guiding Light*
19. Pat Steele, *The Nurses*; Martha Allen, *The Doctors*
20. Bonnie Harmer, *One Life to Live*; Nola Aldrich, *The Doctors*; Echo di Savoy, *One Life to Live*

Mary Stuart (Joanne Tourneur)

Photo by Leslie Murray

12
SEARCH FOR TOMORROW

Twenty Questions

1. Joanne Tourneur and Stu Bergman have been dear friends for decades. Are they distantly related in some way, and, if so, how?

    a. They are related in no way.
    b. Her father and his mother were first cousins.
    c. Their fathers were half-brothers.
    d. Her father married his mother.

2. What did Stu sell for many years before he became a restaurateur?

    a. cars
    b. office supplies
    c. groceries
    d. houses

3. Who fathered Jo's daughter, Patti?

    a. Keith Barron
    b. Victor Barron
    c. Arthur Tate
    d. Wilbur Peabody

THE SOAP OPERA *Digest* SCRAPBOOK

4. *What was the name of Arthur Tate's dedicated lawyer and friend, who carried a torch for Jo?*

    a. Ned Hilton
    b. Nathan Walsh
    c. Phil Nathanson
    d. Ned Walsh

5. *How was Arthur related to the confused Allison Simmons?*

    a. He and Eunice conceived her during his marriage to Jo.
    b. Arthur's aunt, Cornelia, was Allison's mother.
    c. Arthur's first wife, Sue, had Allison by Rex Twining.
    d. They were half-brother and -sister.

6. *Which is not true of Fred Metcalf, Allison's husband?*

    a. He was an alcoholic.
    b. He was a newspaper reporter.
    c. He had a congenital heart condition.
    d. He was dominated by his mother.

7. *Before Jo's courtship with Sam Reynolds, Jo took more than a year to warm up to him. Why the cold shoulder?*

    a. She disapproved of her daughter Patti's relationship with his son, Len.
    b. His ex-wife, Andrea, falsely led Jo to believe he was a womanizer.
    c. Jo blamed Sam for Stu's business failures.
    d. Jo blamed Sam for exerting so much business pressure on Arthur as to cause Arthur's fatal heart attack.

8. *One night Sam told Jo "the secret behind the night of the fire." What was the secret?*

    a. Andrea had staged a fire in order to kidnap Jamie, Len's twin, but Jamie ended up dying in the fire.

SEARCH FOR TOMORROW

    b. Jamie, Len's twin, had died in a fire while Andrea was carrying on with another man.

    c. Jamie, Len's twin, had accidentally set a fire, which Andrea led Len to believe was set by Sam.

    d. Andrea and her lover were trapped in a fire while Jamie was home dying of a fever.

Larry Haines (Stu Bergman)

Photo by Leslie Murray

9. Doug Martin, Eunice's husband, discovered late in life that he had fathered a son, Scott Phillips. How did the boy come by the Phillips name?

    a. Scott's mother concocted a name, "John Phillips," and told Scott he was his late father.

    b. Scott's mother was married to John Phillips when she and Doug conceived Scott.

    c. Scott's mother sold her child to John and Christine Phillips until Scott's grandmother, Ida, located the boy and reared him herself.

    d. Scott's mother gave him up for adoption, and he was then adopted by John and Christine Phillips.

10. Which one of these men was never romantically involved with the seductive Jennifer Pace?

    a. John Wyatt   c. Doug Martin

    b. Scott Phillips   d. Gary Walton

11. How was Janet's first husband, Bud Gardner, related to Jo?

    a. He was her cousin.

    b. He was her nephew through a deceased brother.

    c. He had once been married to her sister Eunice.

    d. He was her half-brother.

12. What caused the death of Janet's second husband, Dan Walton?

    a. a car accident

    b. a fatal blood disease

    c. He fell down a flight of stairs.

    d. He fell up a flight of stairs.

13. Stephanie Wilkins arrived in Henderson as a woman from Tony Vincente's past who tried to wreck his marriage to Jo. What was the story she told Jo about Tony, and was it true?

    a. She had been Tony's first wife's nurse, and when Tony nixed an affair with Stephanie she claimed that Tony poisoned his wife; it was not true.

    b. Stephanie had conceived Wendy by Tony, not by her husband Dave Wilkins; it was not true.

    c. Stephanie's husband, Dave Wilkins, had died under Tony's surgical knife; it was true, but Dave would have expired anyway.

    d. Her husband Dave had an affair with Tony's first wife under Tony's nose, and Tony was too weak to do anything about it; it was true.

SEARCH FOR TOMORROW

14. *Which misfortune has never befallen Jo?*

    a. kidnapped twice
    b. blinded twice
    c. paralyzed after car accident
    d. widowed three times

15. *How did Stephanie come upon the 49-percent share of the Collins Corporation that she spitefully sold to Ted Adamson?*

    a. It was her alimony settlement from her ex, Wade Collins.
    b. It was her alimony settlement from her ex, Wade's brother Clay Collins.
    c. It was an inheritance from Wade and Clay's father, whom Stephanie had treated when she was a nurse.
    d. It was her inheritance from her husband, Clay Collins.

16. *Sunny had long been estranged from her father, Ted, and lived with her mother. What was the last name Sunny used, and where did she get the surname?*

    a. McClure; her mother's maiden name
    b. McCabe; her stepfather's name
    c. McCabe; her mother's maiden name
    d. McClure; her stepfather's name

Jack Betts is probably the consummate villain of the soap world. He was the murderous, sexually warped Dr. Ivan Kipling on *One Life to Live,* **phony art trader Louis St. George on** *Another World,* **and the two-faced tycoon-turned-fugitive Lars Bogard on** *All My Children.* **Ironically, Jack is one of the nicest guys one would ever want to meet!**

Photo by Kacey Associates Inc.

17. Who was the bogus New Orleans psychic involved in the Nick D'Antoni caper?

    a. Tante Helene LeGrande
    b. Tante Helene Leveaux
    c. Tante Lorraine Benard
    d. Tante Lorraine Machaux

18. What forced Spencer Langley to stop falsely assuming the identity of Brian Emerson, Stephanie's son?

    a. He fell for Wendy.
    b. He ached to land Stephanie in the sack.
    c. Brian came to Henderson and ended Spencer's game.
    d. His conscience bothered him because he came to look upon Stephanie and Wendy as the family he never had.

19. Why did Stu's second wife, Ellie, leave Henderson?

    a. She left to nurse her sick aunt.
    b. She went to a hospital for alcoholics.
    c. She ran off with the chef at the Hartford House Inn.
    d. She discovered that her late husband was alive and reconciled with him.

20. What was Travis Sentell's full name?

    a. Roger Travis Sentell
    b. Travis Roger Sentell
    c. Travis Martin Sentell
    d. Travis Tourneur Sentell

SEARCH FOR TOMORROW

Search for Tomorrow Word Search

Soap-related words are hidden in this maze of letters. They read forward, backward, up, down, or diagonally, always in a straight line. Circle the letters as you find them. Letters may be used more than once. The remaining letters will (in order) spell a hidden message. To start, we have indicated the first word in bold type. Enjoy!

```
P  B  R  I  A  N  N  O  S  R  E  D  N  E  H
E  R  S  T  O  N  E  R  O  M  H  S  O  J  M
L  S  E  N  I  A  H  Y  R  R  A  L  I  A  B
U  N  L  G  W  A  R  R  E  N  L  L  R  I  E
S  O  L  R  N  L  R  A  P  E  D  C  G  I  C
O  I  A  U  O  A  S  E  K  A  I  E  N  N
A  T  D  E  T  R  N  S  C  A  L  A  A  A  A
I  C  N  N  S  C  A  T  M  O  H  R  H  T  R
S  U  E  R  I  H  I  C  W  P  U  N  G  S  A
E  R  K  U  N  F  C  E  E  A  O  R  T  I  E
N  T  E  O  A  A  S  T  L  O  M  O  R  R  P
O  S  V  T  B  R  S  T  N  A  R  R  A  K  P
D  N  E  E  M  A  R  Y  S  T  U  A  R  T  A
N  O  T  L  L  E  T  N  E  S  A  Z  I  L  E
I  C  S  U  Z  I  O  W  Y  A  W  A  N  U  R
```

161

THE SOAP OPERA *Digest* SCRAPBOOK

SEARCH FOR TOMORROW
Family Tree 1984

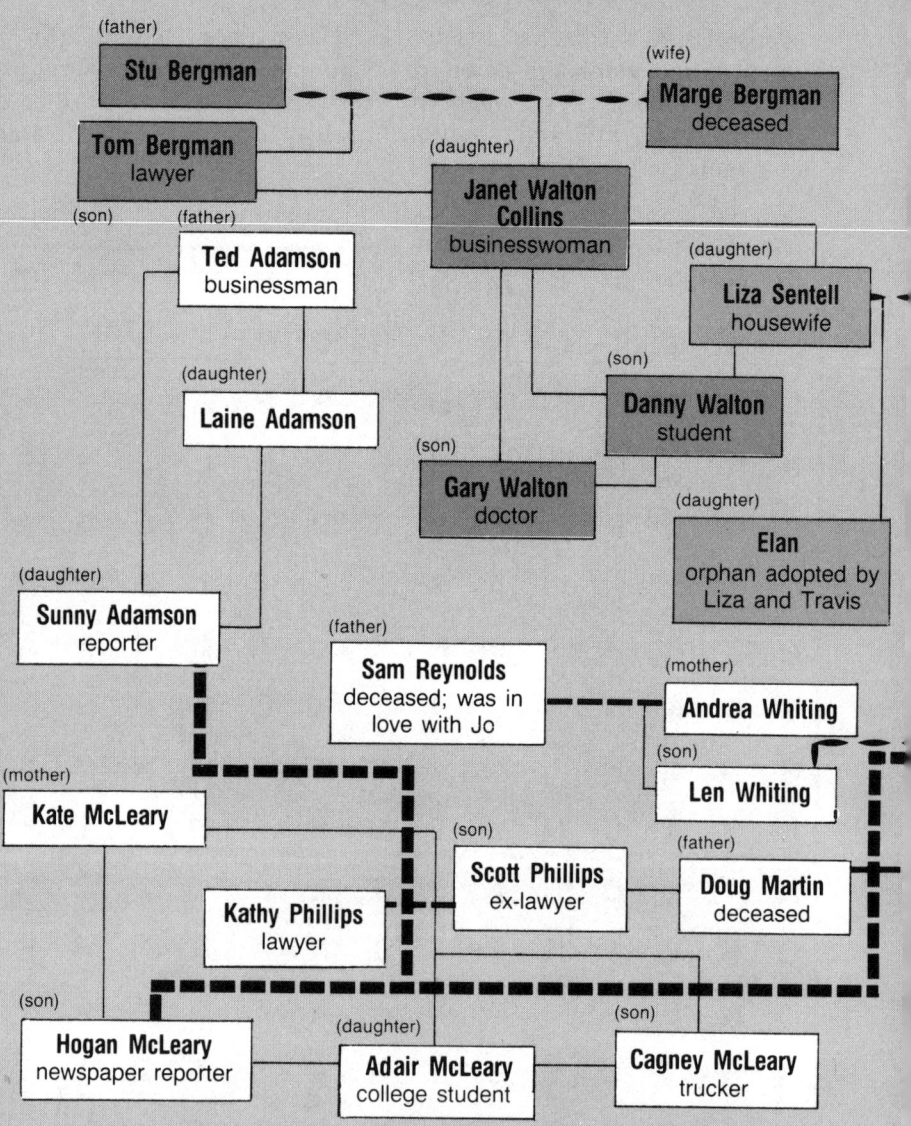

SEARCH FOR TOMORROW

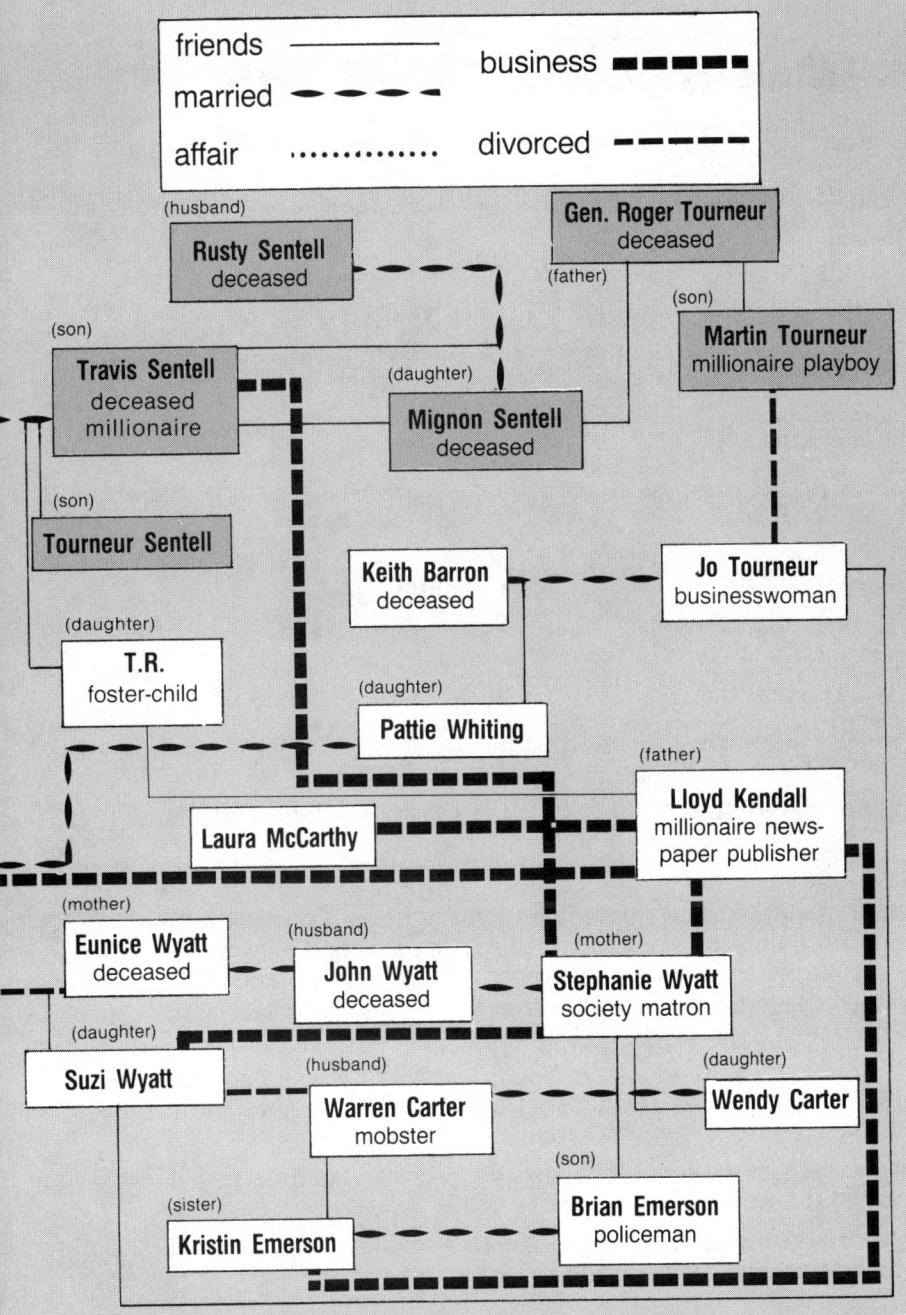

Soaptrivia #12
MOUSTACHE TWIRLERS

Match the dastardly villain with his mountain of misdeeds.

A. Craig Montgomery, *As the World Turns*
B. Alan Spaulding, *Guiding Light*
C. Dr. Ivan Kipling, *One Life to Live*
D. Lars Bogard, *All My Children*
E. Jack Abbott, *The Young and the Restless*
F. Jefferson Brown, *Edge of Night*
G. D. L. Brock, *General Hospital*
H. Garth Slater, *Loving*
I. James Stenbeck, *As the World Turns*
J. Roger Thorpe, *Guiding Light*
K. Dr. John Dixon, *As the World Turns*
L. Alex Marshall, *Days of Our Lives*
M. Warren Carter, *Search for Tomorrow*
N. Warren Andrews, *Guiding Light*
O. Rick Daros, *The Young and the Restless*
P. Bradley Raines, *Guiding Light*
Q. Stefano DiMera, *Days of Our Lives*
R. Richard Fairchild III, *As the World Turns*
S. Gil Barrett, *All My Children*
T. Dane Hammond, *Loving*

1. Impregnated a drug addict who later became a nun; sent his brother flying off a balcony in a scuffle; dumped his lover for her daughter, whom he married; divorced his wife and manipulated his way into her late father's company; became right hand to local white-collar criminals
2. Fought dirty against a local health inspector who closed his sauce factory due to botulism; paid an arsonist to set fire to the factory to collect insurance
3. Allied himself with his ex-boss's illegitimate daughter to outbid the ex-boss in local land deals
4. Held his son and daughter-in-law to a loveless marriage by threatening the life of her lover; faked his own death in order

to commit local murders anonymously; headed an international crime network

5. Resented fellow professionals who came from solid families; knew the true identity of a mystery man; seduced an impressionable young nurse away from her fiancé and entered her into a Svengali-ish marriage; aided a local millionaire in framing the millionaire's romantic rival for a crime

6. Resented fellow professionals who came from solid families; blackmailed one nemesis with the knowledge that his foe's "niece" was really his daughter; raped two of his wives, one of whom he impregnated; kidnapped his son from his ex-wife and nemesis, who had since married; discovered he had a daughter, who later married the son of another professional rival; made countless attempts to frame that rival for moral and professional misconduct; faked his own death to go undercover to catch yet another nemesis in the act of killing him

7. Ran gun rackets out of his own nightclub; married a girl for her money, then seduced and married her best friend

8. Vowed vengeance on his murdered son's scheming lover; tried to kill his own lover's ex-husband; was proven to be a Nazi war criminal

9. Married a girl for her money and tried to kill her lover; was seduced by his boss's oversexed daughter; tried to drain his wife of her finances and sabotage her lover's business projects; faked paralysis to keep his wife by his side; kidnapped his wife's child

10. Raped his stepdaughter; informed the stepdaughter's boyfriend of his true parentage

11. Repeatedly raped his own daughter; turned his fragile wife into an alcoholic and occasionally beat her; tried to kill his daughter's boyfriend; tried to blackmail the boyfriend's father, his professional rival, with knowledge of his extramarital affair

12. Taunted his best friend's wife with obscene phone calls and physical passes; attempted to rape and murder her

13. Shot an innocent man in hopes that the man's arch-nemesis would kill the husband of a beautiful woman with whom this evil genius was obsessed; escaped a mental home and assumed the identity of a friend he had killed in a fire

14. Assumed the identity of a friend he had left for dead after a plane crash; assumed the friend's fortune and position in society; forced a beautiful ballerina to live with him by threatening to reveal her brief flirtation with larceny; killed a wily servant who tried to outsmart him; married an heiress whom he tried to kill when she discovered his misdeeds

15. Was hired by a rich busybody to seduce the daughter-in-law she despised; fell in love with the daughter-in-law, then tried to kill her when he realized she loved someone else; had murdered another girlfriend before

16. Paid a doctor to switch his first wife's dead child with one given up by a woman in the midst of a divorce; bribed a witness to smear his wife's reputation in a custody suit over their son; was blackmailed by a sly young assistant into helping him elude the authorities because of other crimes he committed; ruined his first wife's romance with a heroic lawyer by using their sick son's disapproval of the wife's new union; married the daughter of the lawyer, who proved he was a criminal conspirator; had numerous affairs, one of which produced a daughter who eventually turned against him; arranged to frame another romantic rival for drug possession

17. Impregnated and dumped his boss's daughter; contributed to the breakup of his father's marriage to the mother of the girl he impregnated; tried to seduce the girl's sister-in-law; married and divorced a sympathetic nurse; married the girl he impregnated, then raped her because she loved someone else; had a racy past with his wife's romantic rival, whom he raped and kidnapped; blackmailed someone into helping him make his enemies believe he was dead

18. Continually cheated on his sweet young wife, who finally had the good sense to shoot him; seduced his well-endowed, social-climbing young stepmother; investigated his sister's boyfriend behind her back

19. Made his fragile young wife a physical and emotional puppet; tried to seduce and kill the ex-hooker wife of the man his wife believed she loved; implanted a mind-control device into the brain of the hooker's hubby; patronized hookers, whom he outfitted in black negligees

Michael Zaslow may be a heartthrob as David Renaldi on *One Life to Live*, but his previous character, Roger Thorpe on *Guiding Light*, was a blackmailer, and fugitive. Roger, will live forever as the most multifaceted "heavy" of all time.

20. Married the mother of his child in order to collect an enormous inheritance; had an affair with the girl who groomed his racehorse; became involved in the drug rackets; withheld his discovery that his wife's new love was the rightful heir to his family fortune; almost married the ingenuish ex-wife of his girlfriend's father; tried to kill both the father and his romantic rival

Doug Davidson (Paul Williams) and Steven Ford (Andy Richards)

13
THE YOUNG AND THE RESTLESS

Twenty Questions

1. Which is true of the show's setting, Genoa City?

    a. It is an actual town in Wisconsin.
    b. It is an actual town in Ohio.
    c. It is a fictional town located one hour from Detroit.
    d. It is a fictional town located near the outskirts of Chicago.

2. Stuart Brooks vehemently disapproved of Snapper Foster as a mate for his daughter, Chris. Whom did Stuart want for a son-in-law?

    a. Greg Foster, Snapper's brother
    b. Jed Andrews
    c. Brock Reynolds
    d. Ron Becker

THE SOAP OPERA *Digest* SCRAPBOOK

3. *What did Leslie Brooks name her musically based nightclub?*

    a. The Fermata
    b. The Allegro
    c. The Accelerando
    d. The Sostenuto

4. *What job did Jill hold before she became a seductive gold-digger?*

    a. a barmaid
    b. a factory worker
    c. a hairdresser
    d. a supermarket cashier

5. *Which was* not *true of Brad Eliot, Leslie's first husband?*

    a. He gave up medicine after his fiancée's son died under his scalpel.
    b. He was a psychiatrist.
    c. He was a newspaper reporter.
    d. He was a licensed private detective.

6. *How did Sally McGuire's husband, Pierre Rolland, die?*

    a. He had a stroke after discovering that Snapper fathered Sally's baby.
    b. He was killed by a thug.
    c. He had a heart attack after he discovered that his sister tried to bribe Sally to leave Genoa City.
    d. He was killed in a car accident after finding Sally in bed with Snapper.

7. *What was the name of Liz Foster's errant first husband?*

    a. Cal Foster
    b. Bill Foster
    c. Sam Powers
    d. Charlie Powers

THE YOUNG AND THE RESTLESS

Eileen Davidson
(Ashley Abbott)

8. Which was not true of Jennifer Brooks's old flame, Bruce Henderson?

    a. He was Liz Foster's estranged brother.

    b. He fathered Lauralee Brooks and Mark Henderson.

    c. He ran the family farm.

    d. His wife's name was Regina.

9. Which two Brooks sisters were raped, and who were their respective violators?

    a. Chris, by George Curtis; Peggy, by Ron Becker

    b. Chris, by Ron Becker; Peggy, by Jack Curtis

    c. Lauralee, by Jed Andrews; Chris, by Ron Becker

    d. Leslie, by Jack Curtis; Peggy, by Ron Becker

THE SOAP OPERA *Digest* SCRAPBOOK

10. Which was true of Jill and Brock Reynolds, Kay Chancellor's son?

    a. They had a fling in Paris.

    b. They had a fling in Genoa City, which briefly caused Jill to believe that Brock had fathered her son, Phillip.

    c. They married "in the sight of God" to legitimize Phillip, Jill's son by Phillip Chancellor.

    d. They married legally to legitimize Phillip, Jill's son by Phillip Chancellor, but the marriage was annulled.

11. Which is *not* true of the seductive, scatterbrained Nikki Reed?

    a. Her father tried to rape her.

    b. She had two bouts with obsessive psychos who tried to kill her.

    c. She got involved with a white slavery ring.

    d. She became sexually involved with a religious cult leader.

12. Which of these women never shared a bed with Paul Williams?

    a. Nikki Reed   c. April Stevens

    b. Peggy Brooks   d. Cindy Lake

13. What was the last name of Jonas, Leslie's mysterious friend?

    a. Crown

    b. Falk

    c. Fargo

    d. His last name was never mentioned.

14. Which of these men was never involved romantically with rich, lonely Kay Chancellor?

THE YOUNG AND THE RESTLESS

    a. Stuart Brooks
    b. Derek Thurston
    c. Douglas Austin
    d. Earl Bancroft

15. *How many children do Carl and Mary Williams have?*

    a. two
    b. three
    c. four
    d. five

16. *Who was April Stevens's estranged sister?*

    a. Barbara Ann Harding
    b. Barbara Jean Harding
    c. Barbara Jean Hardy
    d. Barbara Jo Hartig

17. *Where did Victor Newman imprison Michael Scott, Julia's lover, and how did Victor explain Michael's predicament to Paul, whom Victor hired as Michael's guard?*

    a. Victor's attic; Michael was supposedly Victor's deranged brother
    b. Victor's wine cellar; Michael was supposedly his deranged brother-in-law
    c. a specially built cell in Victor's basement; Michael was supposedly Victor's deranged brother-in-law
    d. a specially built cell in Victor's basement; Victor told Paul the truth and paid him big bucks for his secrecy

18. Under what circumstances did Lauralee Prentiss leave Genoa City?

   a. She tricked Victor into returning the company proxies he stole from her ex-husband, Lance, and left in hopes of reconciling with Lance.
   b. She realized she had no future with Lance, who left with Leslie and their child.
   c. She tricked Victor into returning the company proxies he stole from Lance and moved to Europe with Lucas.
   d. She stole the company proxies Victor had in turn stolen from Lance and left to start anew.

19. Which of these women never became one of Jack Abbott's conquests?

   a. Nikki Reed
   b. Jill Foster
   c. Diane Jenkins
   d. Gina Roma

20. Who was Andy Richards's dizzy first wife?

   a. Nikki Reed
   b. Carol Richards
   c. Karen Richards
   d. Carolyn Harper

THE YOUNG AND THE RESTLESS

The Young & the Restless Word Search

Soap-related words are hidden in this maze of letters. They read forward, backward, up, down, or diagonally, always in a straight line. Circle the letters as you find them. Letters may be used more than once. The remaining letters will (in order) spell a hidden message. To start, we have indicated the first word in bold type. Enjoy!

```
N O R E G R E M S I N G E R J
K X J D A V I D S O N E T A A
E A I U R S H D I N A N B E C
C Y Y O L E R A N I G O R R K
N Y D C R I H E M A T A O I A
A E Y O H C A P T C B C T A B
L I E E L A T N O E Y I C L B
L N T C O E N S E T P T I B O
I A F R U N M C N W S Y V G T
E H I O E E Y O E A M I M B T
V P L V T A U T T L D A R A R
R E E I N O L T T T L N N H A
U T C D R E S R T A L O E E C
S S A N O S I L A S P S R R I
A F F A I R L I A M K C A L B
```

THE SOAP OPERA Digest SCRAPBOOK

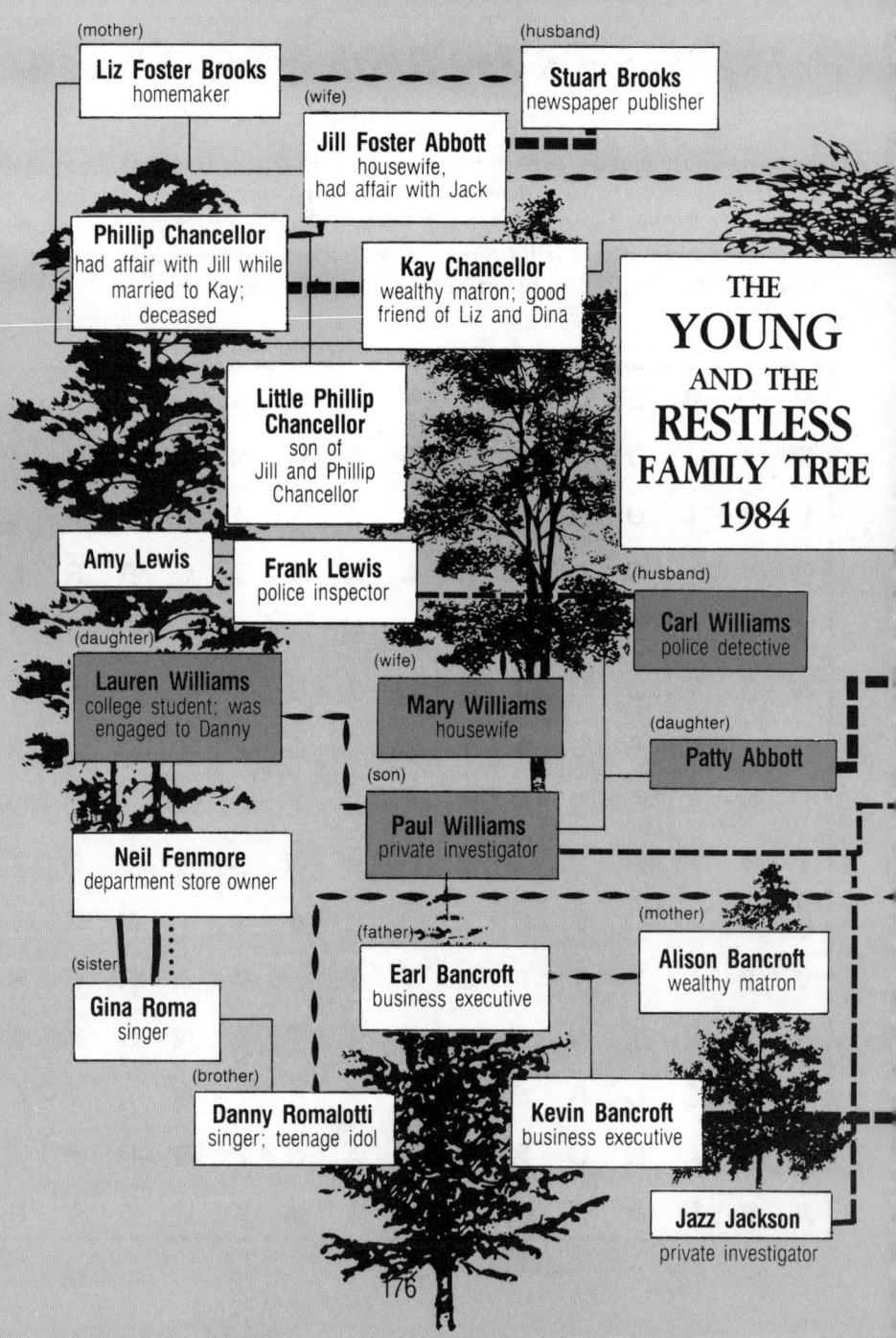

THE YOUNG AND THE RESTLESS FAMILY TREE 1984

- **Liz Foster Brooks** (mother) — homemaker
- **Stuart Brooks** (husband) — newspaper publisher
- **Jill Foster Abbott** (wife) — housewife, had affair with Jack
- **Phillip Chancellor** — had affair with Jill while married to Kay; deceased
- **Kay Chancellor** — wealthy matron; good friend of Liz and Dina
- **Little Phillip Chancellor** — son of Jill and Phillip Chancellor
- **Amy Lewis**
- **Frank Lewis** — police inspector
- **Carl Williams** (husband) — police detective
- **Lauren Williams** (daughter) — college student; was engaged to Danny
- **Mary Williams** (wife) — housewife
- **Patty Abbott** (daughter)
- **Paul Williams** (son) — private investigator
- **Neil Fenmore** — department store owner
- **Earl Bancroft** (father) — business executive
- **Alison Bancroft** (mother) — wealthy matron
- **Gina Roma** (sister) — singer
- **Danny Romalotti** (brother) — singer; teenage idol
- **Kevin Bancroft** — business executive
- **Jazz Jackson** — private investigator

THE YOUNG AND THE RESTLESS

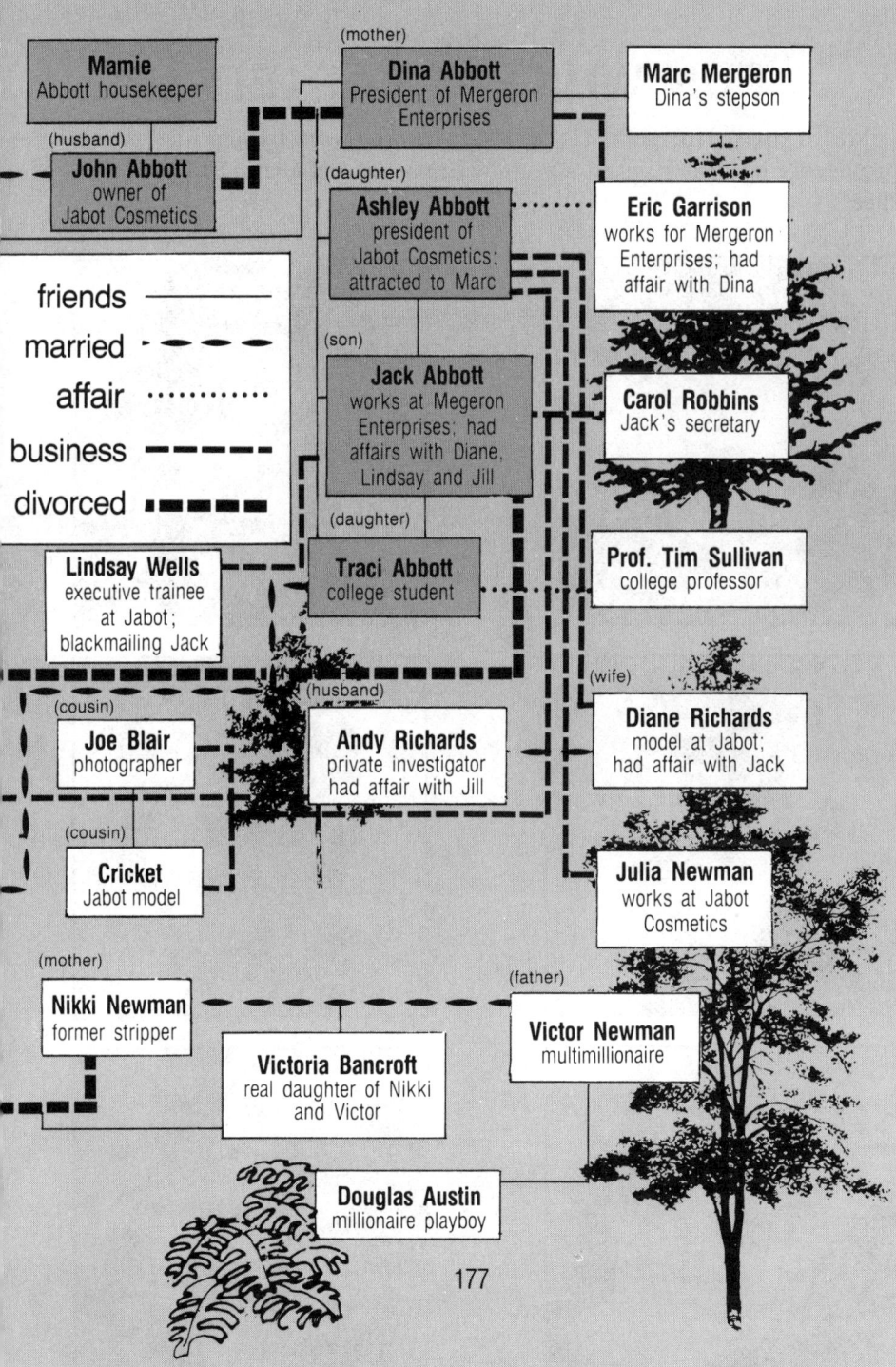

THE **SOAP OPERA** *Digest* SCRAPBOOK

Photoquiz #5
FUN WHILE IT LASTED

Match these former couples who, under various circumstances, provided each other with "tea and sympathy" between the proverbial sheets.

THE SOAP OPERA *Digest* SCRAPBOOK

THE YOUNG AND THE RESTLESS

ANSWERS

All My Children Twenty Questions (page 1)

1. D	5. A	9. D	13. D	17. A
2. A	6. C	10. D	14. C	18. A
3. D	7. A	11. A	15. B	19. B
4. B	8. C	12. B	16. D	20. D

THE SOAP OPERA *Digest* SCRAPBOOK

All My Children Word Search (page 7)

ANGIE
BONKERS
BROOKE CUDAHY
CASINO
CENTER (CITY)
CHANDLERS
CHATEAU
CHUCK (TYLER)
CLIFF (WARNER)
COCAINE
DEVON McFADDEN
DONNA PESCOW
DUKES
ELLEN DALTON
ERICA KANE
FOXY'S
GILLIAN (SPENCER)
GOAL POST
GREG NELSON
JENNY
JESSE (HUBBARD)
LOVE
(MICHAEL) KNIGHT
MONA TYLER
NINA WARNER
PALMER CORTLANDT
RUTH WARRICK
SAM (BRADY)
STAR
STEAMPIT

Hidden message: WELCOME TO PINE VALLEY

Soaptrivia #1:
From Whence They Came, Part I (page 10)

A—6   E—14   I—1   M—12   Q—7
B—3   F—20   J—16   N—4   R—15
C—8   G—18   K—5   O—17   S—2
D—11 H—19   L—9   P—13   T—10

ANSWERS

Another World Twenty Questions (page 13)

1. B
2. D
3. A
4. A
5. A
6. D
7. B
8. A
9. B
10. D
11. B
12. C
13. D
14. A
15. C
16. A
17. B
18. C
19. B
20. A

Another World Word Search (page 19)

ANNA STUART
BAY CITY
BLACKMAIL
BLAINE EWING
BRIBERY
BROOKLYN
CHRIS (RICH)
(CARL) HUTCHINS
CATLIN (EWING)
(DAVID) OLIVER
DEATH
DRUGS
FORTUNE
GAIL (BROWN)
(JAMIE) FRAME
JULIA (SHEARER)
KEVIN (THATCHER)
LINDA DANO
MACKENZIE (CORY)
(MARK) SINGLETON
MARRIAGES
NICOLE (LOVE)
PAUL (STEVENS)
PLANE CRASH
PUBLISHING
ROBERTA FLACK
ROY BINGHAM
(TED) BANCROFT
(TOM) WIGGIN
TRUST FUND
(VICTORIA) WYNDHAM

Hidden message: CAN TRUE LOVE SURVIVE?

THE SOAP OPERA Digest SCRAPBOOK

Photoquiz #1: Better Halves (page 22)

A—7 (Tony and Anna DiMera, *Days of Our Lives*)
B—9 (Ed and Maureen Bauer, *Guiding Light*)
C—4 (Alan and Monica Quartermaine, *General Hospital*)
D—1 (Greg and Jenny Nelson, *All My Children*)
E—8 (Sandy and Blaine Cory, *Another World*)
F—2 (Adam and Erica Chandler, *All My Children*)
G—5 (Gunnar and Barbara Stenbeck, *As the World Turns*)
H—6 (Robert and Holly Scorpio, *General Hospital*)
I—3 (Les and Pat Baxter, *All My Children*)

Soaptrivia #2: Hell Hath No Fury. . . . (page 26)

A—6	E—15	I—8	M—16	Q—11
B—10	F—18	J—14	N—9	R—4
C—5	G—19	K—3	O—17	S—7
D—12	H—20	L—13	P—2	T—1

As the World Turns Twenty Questions (page 31)

1. C	5. A	9. D	13. B	17. B
2. A	6. D	10. A	14. D	18. B
3. D	7. B	11. B	15. D	19. D
4. B	8. D	12. C	16. A	20. C

ANSWERS

As the World Turns Crossword Puzzle
(page 40)

	1 J	2 A	3 B		4 L	5 E	6 N	7 A		8 B	9 O	10 B
11 E	C	R	U		13 A	A	R	O	N	14 T	U	N	E
15 F	A	I	R		16 S	C	O	T	T	17 B	R	Y	C	E
18 F	R	A	N	19 N	I	E	S			20 R	I	S	E	S
21 S	E	N		22 O	D	D		23 S	24 E	A	N			
		25 B	26 L	U	E		27 M	C	N	E	I	L		28 L
29 E	30 L	L	E	N		31 H	E	R	D	S		32 I	33 W	34 O
35 L	E	O	N		36 S	O	D	A	S		37 T	S	A	R
38 I	D	O		39 A	T	R	I	P		40 S	W	A	R	D
		41 M	42 A	R	I	S	A		43 R	O	O	M		
	44 P	Y	R	E		45 B	E	A		46 C	47 A	48 B
49 O	50 P	51 E	R	A		52 P	A	T	R	53 I	C	I	A
54 H	U	G		55 O	56 N	A	P	I	E	R		57 R	O	S	S
58 I	R	O	N		59 G	E	A	R	Y		60 A	L	L	S
61 O	R	S		62 T	A	S	S			63 L	E	O

Soaptrivia #3: Fill in the Blanks (page 44)

1. Nola Madison
2. *Register*
3. *Titan*
4. Cindy Clark Matthews
5. Farley Granger
6. Martha Marceau; Bill Marceau
7. William Gray Espy; Snapper
8. Jacqueline Brookes; Beatrice Gordon; Sally Frame

THE SOAP OPERA *Digest* SCRAPBOOK

9. Gloria Monty
10. Ben Harper; *Love of Life*
11. Shelly Granger; Phil Dade; Trey Clegg
12. Johnny Forbes; Roger Forbes; Amelia Whitley; prostitution
13. Marge; Janet; Tom; "Junior"
14. Kimberly Beaulac; Michael Pavel; Ryan Fenelli
15. Ken; Andrew
16. *The Secret Storm*; 20
17. Barbara; Alan; Carlson; Winfield; Rosehill
18. *Chronicle*; Jennifer; Leslie; Lauralee; Chris; Peggy
19. Clayton; Ann
20. *General Hospital*

Capitol Twenty Questions (page 47)

1. B	5. D	9. D	13. B	17. C
2. B	6. A	10. A	14. D	18. A
3. B	7. C	11. C	15. A	19. B
4. A	8. A	12. D	16. C	20. A

Capitol Word Search (page 53)

ALDEN
CAMPAIGNS
CLEGGS
CONSTANCE (TOWERS)
DAVID (MASON DANIELS)
DAWN (PARRISH)
(ED) NELSON
ENTERPRISES
JEFFERSONIA
JULIE (McCANDLESS)
(KIMBERLY) ROSS
LANA WOOD
(LESLIE) GRAVES
(MATT) McCANDLESS
MURDOCH
MYRNA
(NICHOLAS) WALKER
(PAULA) DENNING
POLITICS
RICHARD (EGAN)
RORY CALHOUN
SKIING
SLOANE (DENNING)
TODD (CURTIS)
(TODD) STARKS
THOMAS (McCANDLESS)
TONJA (WALKER)
UNIVERSITY
WALLY (McCANDLESS)
WASHINGTON
ZED DIAMOND
ZURICH

Hidden message: POLITICAL INTRIGUE

ANSWERS

Soaptrivia #4: What a Way to Go (page 56)

A—10	E—12	I—11	M—13	Q—9
B—6	F—15	J—5	N—1	R—19
C—8	G—2	K—20	O—3	S—18
D—17	H—16	L—4	P—14	T—7

Days of Our Lives Twenty Questions
(page 59)

1. C	5. D	9. C	13. B	17. A
2. B	6. A	10. D	14. C	18. C
3. A	7. B	11. D	15. B	19. D
4. B	8. A	12. A	16. C	20. C

Days of Our Lives Crossword Puzzle
(page 64)

THE SOAP OPERA *Digest* SCRAPBOOK

Photoquiz #2: Far from the Tree (page 68)

A—1 (Karen Dixon/Cynthia Haines, *As the World Turns*)
B—13 (Brad/Naomi Vernon, *One Life to Live*)
C—7 (Mike/Bill Bauer, *Guiding Light*)
D—8 (Jordy/Sam Clegg, *Capitol*)
E—9 & 15 (Tad Martin/Opal and Ray Gardner, *All My Children*)
F—4 (Quinton/Henry Chamberlain, *Guiding Light*)
G—9 & 15 (Jenny Nelson/Opal and Ray Gardner, *All My Children*)
H—12 (Liza Sentell/Janet Collins, *Search for Tomorrow*)
I—3 (Sloane Clegg/Mark Denning, *Capitol*)
J—6 (Liz Curtis/Kellam Chandler, *Days of Our Lives*)
K—5 (Cecile/Elena dePoulignac, *Another World*)
L—14 (Amanda Spaulding/Jennifer Richards, *Guiding Light*)
M—2 (Angie Hubbard/Pat Baxter, *All My Children*)
N—11 (Sunny/Ted Adamson, *Search for Tomorrow*)
O—10 (James Frame/Rachel Cory, *Another World*)

Soaptrivia #5: They Had to Start Somewhere (page 73)

A—9	E—1 & 15	I—18	M—10	Q—12
B—6 & 11	F—7	J—5 & 11	N—1 & 14	R—13
C—7	G—2	K—6	O—4	S—3
D—9 & 14	H—3	L—5 & 8	P—7	T—5

ANSWERS

Edge of Night Twenty Questions (page 75)

1. A	5. A	9. A	13. D	17. A
2. B	6. A	10. A	14. B	18. D
3. B	7. C	11. A	15. C	19. C
4. D	8. B	12. C	16. A	20. C

Edge of Night Word Search (page 81)

CAMPUS
CHRIS (EGAN)
(JACK) **BOYD**
DEREK MALLORY
DIDI STONER
(ANN) **FLOOD**
(MATTHEW) **GANTZ**
(SANDY) **FAISON**
FORREST
 (COMPTON)
GERALDINE SAXON
GUNTHER WAGNER
IMAGE INC
IRVING ALLEN (LEE)
JASON (ZIMBLER)
KERRY
 (ARMSTRONG)
LARKIN (MALLOY)
LOGAN SWIFT
MILES CAVANAUGH
MITZI (MARTIN)
MONTICELLO
MOTHERHOOD
MYSTERY
PREACHER
PUBLISHING
RUSS (POWELL)
SHARON GABET
SHELLEY (FRANKLYN)
SORORITY
(JODY) **TRAVIS**

Hidden message: AT THE EDGE OF OUR SEATS

Soaptrivia #6: The Official Rogues' Gallery of Monticello (page 84)

A—6	C—9	E—1	G—2	I—4
B—10	D—8	F—7	H—3	J—5

THE SOAP OPERA *Digest* SCRAPBOOK

General Hospital Twenty Questions
(page 87)

1. C	5. D	9. C	13. B	17. B
2. B	6. A	10. D	14. A	18. D
3. A	7. B	11. B	15. B	19. A
4. D	8. A	12. D	16. A	20. D

General Hospital Crossword Puzzle
(page 92)

Soaptrivia #7: How Soon We Forget
(page 96)

A—17—e	E—5—h	I—19—i	M—16—n	Q—1—m
B—10—l	F—13—o	J—7—a	N—20—t	R—15—f
C—8—b	G—4—k	K—18—g	O—12—q	S—6—p
D—11—r	H—9—d	L—2—c	P—14—s	T—3—j

Guiding Light Twenty Questions (page 101)

1. A	5. B	9. B	13. D	17. A
2. C	6. B	10. A	14. B	18. D
3. C	7. C	11. A	15. D	19. C
4. D	8. C	12. B	16. A	20. C

Guiding Light Crossword Puzzle (page 106)

	1 P	2 I	3 E			4 J	5 E	6 E	7 P			8 R	9 E	10 D
11 T	I	R	E		12 L	A	N	N	A		13 G	E	R	E
14 A	L	E	K	15 S	A	N	D	E	R		16 A	V	I	S
17 D	O	N		18 T	R	E	S		19 K	20 O	Z	A	K	
21 S	T	E	22 W	A	R	T		23 B	E	V	E	L		
			24 A	N	Y		25 V	E	R	A		26 E	27 V	28 A
29 T	30 R	31 A	Y	S		32 J	A	R	S			33 W	E	D
34 I	A	N	S			35 A	N	T			36 L	I	E	D
37 N	I	N			38 A	M	E	S		39 F	U	S	S	Y
40 A	N	A		41 O	N	E	S		42 L	I	L			
		43 B	44 I	R	D	S		45 N	I	E	L	46 S	47 E	48 N
	49 P	E	T	E	R		50 F	E	E	L		51 A	V	A
52 N	O	L	A		53 E	54 L	L	E	N	D	55 O	L	A	N
56 N	E	L	S		57 W	O	O	D	S		58 D	A	N	A
59 E	T	E			60 S	U	E	S			61 E	D	S	

Soaptrivia #8: Where's Home? (page 111)

A—7—f & l	D—5—o	F—13—j	H—1—b & i	J—11—e
B—4—k	E—9—h & p	G—15—a	I—3—c	K—2—d
C—10—g & n				

THE SOAP OPERA *Digest* SCRAPBOOK

Unmatched Choices:

6. Denison, Maryland, was the fictional setting of the television version of *Young Doctor Malone* (NBC, 1958-63).
8. Rosehill, New York, was the fictional setting for *Love of Life* (CBS) from 1958 to 1980—the majority of that show's run.
12. Madison, Massachusetts, was the fictional setting of *The Doctors* (NBC) from 1976 to 1982. For the show's first 13 years a town name was never mentioned. (Ditto *General Hospital*, where the setting was not defined as Port Charles, New York, until 1976.)
14. Strathfield was the fictional setting of *From These Roots* (NBC, 1958-61).
m. The Coach House is the main restaurant on *The Edge of Night*.

Loving Twenty Questions (page 113)

1. B	5. B	9. B	13. B	17. B
2. A	6. C	10. C	14. A	18. A
3. D	7. A	11. A	15. D	19. D
4. D	8. C	12. B	16. D	20. B

Loving Word Search (page 119)

ALCOHOLISM
BILLY (BRISTOW)
(CURTIS) **ALDEN**
FATHER JIM
  (VOCHEK)
INCEST
JACK FORBES
JAMES KIBERD
JENNIFER ASHE
JUNE SLATER

(LAUREN-MARIE)
  TAYLOR
LILY (SLATER)
MARILYN (McINTYRE)
MERRILL (VOCHEK)
MURDER
PETER BROWN
PSYCHODRAMA
RAPE
RITA (MAE BRISTOW)
(RON) **TURNER**

SHANA SLOANE
SHANNON EUBANKS
STACEY (DONOVAN)
SUSAN (WALTERS)
TERI KEANE
TOM LIGON
TONY PERELLI
VETERAN
WARREN (HODGES)
(WESLEY) **ADDY**

Hidden message: LOVING EVERY MINUTE

ANSWERS

Soaptrivia #9: Miscellaneous Trivia
(page 122)

1. Karr and Drake
2. Tom Clarkson
3. Steve Burke; Bernard Grant
4. Adam Thorpe
5. Sheilah Rafferty
6. Ann Williams
7. Malcolm Groome
8. Olivia Brandeis Henderson
9. Beth Maynard
10. Elaine
11. Beau Richardson
12. Both roles were played by Anthony Call.
13. Jordan Clarke, who later played Billy Lewis on the same show
14. Mary Matthews; Virginia Dwyer
15. *As the World Turns*
16. Cathy Craig
17. five; India Bishop, Jessica Buchanan, Lenore Curtin, Iris Carrington, Olivia
18. Sonia Petrovna
19. Bruno Wagner
20. Kevin McGuinnes
21. Genie Ann Francis
22. ceramics
23. James Luisi; Iris Carrington
24. Stephen Yates, who later played James Frame on *Another World*

THE SOAP OPERA Digest SCRAPBOOK

25. Carol Ann and Dawn
26. three; Chuck Tyler, Phil Brent, Jim Jefferson
27. *Love Is a Many Splendored Thing*; Marion Hiller
28. Wings Hauser
29. alcoholism; Kay Chancellor
30. three; Christopher Wines, Charles Frank, James O'Sullivan; Erica Kane, Mary Kennicott, Christina Karras
31. a sterling rose
32. Elizabeth Taylor
33. Luke's pearl stickpin and Laura's earring
34. Sam Groom
35. Erica Kane worked for all three and had affairs with them as well
36. Claxton, Wyoming
37. Nancy McGowan; Rose
38. Richardson
39. two; Mary Page Keller, Ariane Munker
40. Pamela Lincoln; Darryl Hickman

One Life to Live Twenty Questions
(page 125)

1. D	5. D	9. C	13. C	17. B
2. A	6. A	10. A	14. B	18. D
3. D	7. A	11. D	15. A	19. A
4. C	8. D	12. B	16. A	20. C

ANSWERS

One Life to Live Crossword Puzzle
(page 130)

	1	2	3	4		5	6	7	8		9	10	11
	A	S	T	A		S	E	A	L		D	E	E
12	A	R	L	E	N	13 T	E	R	R	I	14 E	A	R
15 S	C	O	T	T	|16 A	P	R	I	L	|17 A	V	A
18 A	S	P		19 H	20 A	R	T			21 L	22 A	N	E	S
			23 H	O	R	A		24 M	25 A	I	N			
	26 E	27 R	I	N	S		28 S	A	M	A	N	29 T	30 H	31 A
	32 R	E	L	Y		33 A	L	L	E	N		34 H	A	L
35 G	I	R	L	|36 D	I	E	T	S	|37 A	R	R	S
38 A	K	A	|39 C	A	R	E	Y	|40 O	V	E	R	
41 D	A	N |42 W	O	L	E	K	|43 S	N	O	W	Y	
		|44 I	R	E	D	|45 C	R	E	W			
46 S	47 L	48 A	T	E		49 F	O	O	L		50 D	51 A	52 D
53 L	I	L		54 L	55 O	56 U	I	S		57 I	58 M	A	G	E
59 E	V	E	|60 L	A	R	R	Y	|61 F	A	H	E	Y
62 D	E	C	|63 I	T	E	M		|64 E	E	L	S	

Photoquiz #3: Mom Always Liked You Best (page 134)

A—3 (Blaine and Larry Ewing, *Another World*)

B—7 (Joe and Paul Martin, *All My Children*)

C—4 (Ross and Justin Marler, *Guiding Light*)

D—10 (Bobbie and Luke Spencer, *General Hospital*)

E—1 (Floyd and Katie Parker, *Guiding Light*)

F—5 (Stacey and Cass Winthrop, *Another World*)

G—8 (Trish and Josh Lewis, *Guiding Light*)

H—11 (Larry and Anna Wolek, *One Life to Live*)
I—6 (Ed and Quinn Harding, *Another World*)
J—9 (Roger and Jillian Coleridge, *Ryan's Hope*)
K—2 (Nola and Tony Reardon, *Guiding Light*)

Soaptrivia #10: True or False? (page 138)

1. True.
2. True.
3. False. The lady's name was Helen Murdock.
4. False. They are brother and sister.
5. True.
6. False. They grew up on a farm in Oklahoma.
7. True.
8. False. Gifford played Keith's father, Senator Gordon Whitney.
9. True.
10. False. It was Ed Power.
11. True, as Tom Hughes.
12. False. It was Christopher Walken.
13. True.
14. True.
15. True.
16. False. Her name is Delia.
17. False. His half-sister is Vanessa Chamberlain.
18. False. His name was Denver Hobson.
19. False. Her sister is Rita Stapleton.
20. False. She deliberately tried to break them up.

ANSWERS

Ryan's Hope Twenty Questions (page 141)

1. C	5. D	9. C	13. D	17. C
2. A	6. B	10. A	14. B	18. A
3. C	7. C	11. B	15. B	19. B
4. A	8. A	12. B	16. C	20. C

Ryan's Hope Word Search (page 147)

ANTRA
(GLORIA) DEHAVEN
(MAX) DUBUJAEK
EXPLOSION
(JACK) FENELLI
FLASH
FRANK RYAN
(ROBIN) GREER
(EARL) HINDMAN
(SCOTT) HOLMES
JACQUELINE
   (NOVAK)
JAIL
JOE NOVAK
JOHNNY (RYAN)
KENNY (GRAHAM)
(LEIGH) KIRKLAND
LAUREN (O'BRYAN)
MAEVE (RYAN)
MAFIA
MAGGIE (SHELBY)
NANCY ADDISON
NEW YORK CITY
(LASLO) NOVOTNY
PREGNANT
PRUDENCE
   (SHEPHARD)
ROGER COLERIDGE
SENECA BEAULAC
SIOBHAN
   (RYAN NOVAK)
SWITZERLAND

Hidden message: THE BIG APPLE ADVENTURE

Photoquiz #4: Thanks for the Memory (page 150)

A—4 (Erica and Tom Cudahy, *All My Children*)

B—7 (Rick and Lesley Webber, *General Hospital*)

C—1 (Kelly and Morgan Nelson, *Guiding Light*)

D—5 (Julia and Victor Newman, *The Young and the Restless*)

E—2 (Brian and Iris Bancroft, *Another World*)

F—3 (Alan and Hope Spaulding, *Guiding Light*)

G—6 (Kim and Nick Andropolous, *As the World Turns*)

THE SOAP OPERA *Digest* SCRAPBOOK

Soaptrivia #11: From Whence They Came, Part II (page 152)

A—10	E—3	I—8	M—17	Q—11
B—7	F—15	J—19	N—4	R—1
C—13	G—5	K—2	O—14	S—9
D—12	H—16	L—20	P—18	T—6

Search for Tomorrow Twenty Questions
(page 155)

1. D	5. B	9. A	13. B	17. B
2. A	6. C	10. C	14. C	18. A
3. A	7. D	11. A	15. D	19. C
4. B	8. B	12. B	16. A	20. D

Search for Tomorrow Word Search
(page 161)

BIGELOWES
BRIAN (EMERSON)
CONSTRUCTION
HENDERSON
INDONESIA
(JOHN) ANISTON
JOSH MORENO
KRISTAN (CARTER)
LARRY HAINES
LAURA (McCARTHY)
(LISA) PELUSO
LIZA SENTELL
MARCIA McCABE
MARY STUART
(PETER) HASKELL
PREGNANT
RAPED
REAPPEARANCE
(ROD) ARRANTS
RUNAWAY
STEPHANIE (WYATT)
STEVE KENDALL
SUZI (CARTER)
TOURNEUR
WARREN (CARTER)

Hidden message: STILL SEARCHING FOR TOMORROW

ANSWERS

Soaptrivia #12: Moustache Twirlers
(page 164)

A—9	E—18	I—20	M—7	Q—4
B—16	F—14	J—17	N—5	R—13
C—19	G—2	K—6	O—15	S—12
D—8	H—11	L—1	P—10	T—3

The Young & the Restless Twenty Questions (page 169)

1. A	5. D	9. A	13. D	17. C
2. A	6. B	10. C	14. A	18. D
3. B	7. B	11. D	15. C	19. A
4. C	8. C	12. B	16. A	20. C

The Young & the Restless Word Search
(page 175)

AFFAIR
ALISON (BANCROFT)
AMY LEWIS
BLACKMAIL
BRENDA (DICKSON)
CHRISTOPHER
  (HOLDER)
DINA (ABBOTT)
DIVORCE
(EILEEN) DAVIDSON
FACELIFT
GENOA CITY
GINA
JABOT COSMETICS
JACK ABBOTT
(JOE) BLAIR
JULIA NEWMAN
KAY CHANCELLOR
MARLA (ADAMS)
MELODY (THOMAS)
MERGERON
  (ENTERPRISES)
PATTY (ABBOTT)
SCOTT (PALMER)
SINGER
ST. CROIX
STEPHANIE
  (WILLIAMS)
STEVEN (FORD)
SURVEILLANCE
TRACI (ABBOTT)
VICTOR (NEWMAN)

Hidden message: THEY MAY BE YOUNG BUT NOT RESTLESS

THE SOAP OPERA *Digest* SCRAPBOOK

Photoquiz #5: Fun While It Lasted
(page 178)

A—12 (Becky and Bo, *One Live to Live*)

B—7 (Doug and Merrill, *Loving*)

C—5 (Rae and Michael, *Ryan's Hope*)

D—13 (Luke and Holly, *General Hospital*)

E—4 (Alex and Marie, *Days of Our Lives*)

F—1 (Sunny and Lee, *Search for Tomorrow*)

G—10 (Clarice and Robert, *Another World*)

H—6 (Craig and Diana, *As the World Turns*)

I—11 (Bobbie and Scotty, *General Hospital*)

J—2 (Jill and Derek, *The Young and the Restless*)

K—8 (Chris and Amanda, *Days of Our Lives*)

L—3 (Mike and Shana, *Loving*)

M—9 (Rachel and Mitch, *Another World*)

INDEX

Abbott, Ashley, 172, 177
Abbott, Dina, 177
Abbott, Jack, 164, 174, 177
Abbott, Jill Foster, 26, 174, 176
Abbott, John, 177
Abbott, Patty, 176
Abbott, Traci, 177
Adamson, Laine, 162
Adamson, Sunny, 159, 162
Adamson, Ted, 159, 162
Addison, Wayne, 15
Addy, Wesley, 112
Alden, Cabot, 45, 112, 113, 116, 120
Alden, Clayton, 121
Alden, Curtis, 10, 116, 118, 121
Alden, Gwyneth, 121
Alden, Isabelle, 45, 112, 121, 152
Alden, Shana, 115
Aldrin, Greta, 37

Alexander, Nadine, 76
Allan, Jed, 10
Allen, Liz Fraser, 152
Altman, Nancy Addison, 140
Ames, Valerie Hill, 99
Anderson, Bob, 61
Anderson, Mary, 62
Anderson, Melissa, 66
Anderson, Nels, 43
Anderson, Phyllis, 62
Anderson, Ruby, 94
Anderson, Russ, 2
Andrews, Celia, 94
Andrews, Grant, 94
Andrews, Warren, 10, 108
Andropolous, Betsy, 42
Andropolous, Diana, 42
Andropolous, Frank, 42
Andropolous, Steve, 38, 42

THE SOAP OPERA *Digest* SCRAPBOOK

Angelo, Ronnie, 48, 51, 52, 54
Arnett, Terri, 94
Arrants, Rod, 98
Ashley, Pat, 127, 153
Astin, Patty Duke, 73
Austin, Douglas, 173, 177

Bachman, Lisbeth, 49
Backus, Richard, 98
Bailey, Mel, 61
Baker, Jeff, 32
Baldwin, Gail, 86, 95, 152
Baldwin, Lee, 86, 88, 95
Baldwin, Scotty, 88, 95
Baldwin, Tom, 89, 91, 95
Ballard, Diane, 104
Bancroft, Alison, 139, 176
Bancroft, Brian, 10, 21
Bancroft, Earl, 173, 176
Bancroft, Kevin, 176
Bancroft, Victoria, 177
Banning, Bruce, 101
Banning, David, 62, 63, 67
Banning, Janet, 59
Banning, Julie, 62, 63
Banning, Scott, 59, 63, 67
Bannon, Natalie, 37
Barclay, Tony, 8
Barnes, Joanne, 63
Barr, Jordan, 61
Barr, Julia, 5
Barrett, Gil, 4, 164
Barrington, Lawrence, 48, 49
Barron, Keith, 163
Barrow, Bernard, 10
Barry, Patricia, 98
Barton, Jean, 63
Bauer, Bert, 100, 102, 103, 108
Bauer, Bill, 57, 104, 108
Bauer, Charita, 100
Bauer, Charlotte, 103, 104
Bauer, Ed, 10, 102, 103, 105, 108
Bauer, Hillary, 108
Bauer, Hope, 102, 105
Bauer, Leslie, 104
Bauer, Maureen, 109
Bauer, Meta, 101, 104
Bauer, Mike, 102, 103, 108, 110, 139
Bauer, Rick, 108
Baxter, Laura, 153
Beatty, Warren, 73
Beaulac, Kimberly Harris, 144, 146

Beaulac, Nell, 142
Beaulac, Seneca, 10, 141, 142, 149
Bergman, Marge, 162
Bergman, Stu, 162
Bergman, Tom, 162
Beaumont, Helen, 138
Benedict, Henry, 102, 103
Benedict-White, Aristotle, 144
Bennett, Joan, 98
Benson, Jim, 11
Bentley, Meg, 88
Bergman, Stu, 45, 157
Besch, Bibi, 98
Betts, Jack, 159
Beyers, Bill, 49
Bingham, Henrietta, 20
Bingham, Roy, 20
Birney, David, 73
Blaine, Meg, 152
Blair, Carl, 2
Blair, Joe, 177
Blake, Ginny, 95
Blake, Matthew, 17
Blake, Mitch, 17, 44
Blythe, Darren, 90
Bockman, Lisbeth, 54
Bogard, Lars, 159, 164
Borel, Carla, 98
Bowden, Alex, 102
Bradford, Eugene, 66
Bradford, Trista, 66
Brady, Bo, 63, 66, 128
Brady, Carrie, 66
Brady, Kayla, 63, 66
Brady, Maggie, 48, 55
Brady, Marlena, 66
Brady, Roman, 63
Brady, Sam, 8
Brady, Shawn, 66
Brand, Steffi, 95
Brando, Rose, 34
Brandt, Erica, 98
Brannigan, Tim, 11
Brennan, Franny, 35
Brent, Charlie, 8
Brent, Philip, 1, 3, 8
Brewer, Jessie, 89, 95
Brewer, Phil, 89
Bridges, Lloyd, 44
Briskin, Dan, 122
Bristow, Billy, 114, 120
Bristow, Rita Mae, 114, 118, 120

INDEX

Britton, Paul, 11
Brock, D. L., 94, 164
Brock, Dan, 94
Brooks, Chris, 169
Brooks, Jennifer, 56, 171
Brooks, Jonathan, 109
Brooks, Lauralee, 171
Brooks, Leslie, 170
Brooks, Liz Foster, 170, 176
Brooks, Mark, 60
Brooks, Peggy, 172
Brooks, Sal, 144
Brooks, Stuart, 45, 169, 173, 176
Brown, Jefferson, 77, 122, 164
Brown, Susan, 86, 97, 152
Bruder, Patricia, 36
Bruns, Mona, 99
Buchanan, Asa, 128, 132
Buchanan, Becky Abbott, 133
Buchanan, Bo, 127, 132
Buchanan, Clint, 132
Buchanan, Delila, 132
Buchanan, Drew, 132
Buchanan, Olympia, 128, 132
Buchanan, Viki, 122, 124, 125, 132
Burke, Amy, 50
Burke, Fran, 50, 52
Burstyn, Ellen, 73
Burton, Warren, 10

Call, Anthony, 10
Callison, Cassie, 132
Callison, Dorian, 126, 128, 132, 152
Callison, Herb, 10, 132
Cameron, David, 75
Campbell, Flora, 98
Campbell, Kay, 153
Canary, David, 10, 15
Cannell, Julian, 11
Cannell, Kate Thornton, 153
Capice, Louise, 75
Capice, Phil, 75, 77, 78
Carey, MacDonald, 72
Carpenter, John, 11
Carr, John, 11
Carrington, Dennis, 16, 138, 139
Carrington, Eliot, 16
Carrington, Iris, 15
Carson, Constance, 152
Carter, Warren, 163
Carter, Wendy, 163
Carver, Abe, 66

Cassadine, Helena, 123
Cassen, Claire, 34
Cassen, Doug, 34
Carter, Dixie, 122
Carter, Warren, 164
Cavanaugh, Miles, 10, 83
Cavanaugh, Nicole, 76
Chamberlain, Henry, 105, 109
Chamberlain, Nola, 26, 109
Chamberlain, Quint, Jr., 109
Chamberlain, Quinton, 109
Chamberlain, Vanessa, 105
Chancellor, Kay, 172, 176
Chancellor, Phillip, 172, 176
Chandler, Adam, 9, 10
Chandler, Erica, 9
Chandler, Ross, 10
Chandler, Stuart, 9
Chapin, Laurel, 133
Charleson, Leslie, 152
Charleton, Senator, 127
Chernak, Pete, 11
Christopher, Cookie, 122
Clark, Ted, 14
Clayton, Jack, 61
Clayton, Jeri, 61
Clayton, Ted, 56, 122
Clayton, Tina, 128
Clayton, Trish, 61
Clegg, Brenda, 51, 52, 55
Clegg, Jordy, 49, 50, 55
Clegg, Myrna, 26, 44, 47, 48, 50, 55
Clegg, Sam, 48, 50, 55
Clegg, Sloane, 55
Clegg, Trey, 48, 50, 55
Clinton, Brooke, 88
Colby, Larry, 8
Colby, Liza, 3, 8, 26
Colby, Marion, 8
Cole, Tim, 33
Coleridge, Delia, 139, 143, 149
Coleridge, Ed, 143
Coleridge, Faith, 144
Coleridge, Jillian, 142, 149
Coleridge, Roger, 141, 142, 149
Collins, Clay, 159
Collins, Janet Walton, 162
Collins, Wade, 159
Compton, Forrest, 77
Connors, Dorothy, 42
Connors, Jay, 42
Conway, Linell, 103-4

THE SOAP OPERA *Digest* SCRAPBOOK

Conway, Marion, 104
Copeland, Joan, 98
Cord, Steven, 11
Corelli, Gary, 133
Correll, Beth, 83
Cortlandt, Daisy, 9, 153
Cortlandt, Donna, 9
Cortlandt, Palmer, 1, 4, 9, 10
Cory, Amanda, 20
Cory, Baby Alexander, 20
Cory, Mackenzie, 10, 12, 14, 15, 18, 20, 44
Cory, Rachel, 20, 26, 44, 153
Cory, Sandy, 20
Coster, Nicholas, 10, 98
Courtney, Jaqueline, 152
Craig, Cathy, 125
Craig, Don, 10, 67, 123
Craig, Donna, 63
Craig, Jim, 125
Crandall, Doris, 102
Cranmer, Melinda, 128
Crawford, Christina, 45
Crawford, Joan, 45
Crawford, Maggie, 42
Crothers, Joel, 10, 98
Cryer, David, 97
Cudahy, Brooke, 4, 5, 9
Cudahy, Tom, 3, 9, 10
Curtin, Lenore, 15
Curtin, Walter, 14, 15
Curtis, Jack, 11
Curtis, Liz, 66
Curtis, Marie, 67
Curtis, Neil, 10, 60, 61, 67

Dabney, Augusta, 96, 97, 112, 152
Dade, Joan, 48
Dade, Phil, 48, 49
Dailey, Irene, 12
Dalton, Ellen, 6, 9
Dalton, Mark, 9
Dancy, Jerry, 97
Dane, Marco, 127, 133
Dante, Mark, 89
D'Antoni, Nick, 160
Daros, Rick, 164
Davidson, Doug, 168
Davidson, Eileen, 171
Davies, Blair, 97
Davies, Gwen, 66
Davis, Nick, 1, 123
Davis, Rachel, 153

Davis, Todd, 89
Dawson, Howard, 88
Dayton, Hal, 55
DeCosgrove, Tie, 16
Delaney, Robert, 11, 14, 122
Delmar, Tracy, 103
Denning, Mark, 50, 55
Denning, Paula, 26, 50, 52, 55
Denning, Sloane, 50
DePoulignac, Cecile, 21, 26, 153
DePoulignac, Elena, 17, 138
Devon, Miss, 21
Diamond, Zed, 52, 55
Dillman, Marty, 103
DiMera, Anna, 66
DiMera, Daphne, 66
DiMera, Stefano, 63, 66, 138, 164
DiMera, Tony, 63, 66
Dixon, Andy, 43
Dixon, John, 35, 37, 43, 164
Dixon, Karen, 26, 39, 43
Donahue, Tony, 45
Donato, Danny, 48, 54
Donovan, Ariel, 43
Donovan, Burke, 39
Donovan, Douglas, 115, 120
Donovan, Dustin, 39, 43, 120
Donovan, Mike, 115, 118, 120
Donovan, Noreen, 117, 120, 152
Donovan, Patrick, 118, 120
Donovan, Rose, 44, 114, 118, 120, 153
Donovan, Stacey, 118, 120
Donahue, Troy, 44
Dorn, Eliot, 77, 78
Dorn, Margo Huntington, 122
Dorrance, Eddie, 11
Downs, Ernie, 18
Drake, Adam, 77, 122
Drake, Julian, 90
Drake, Martin, 90
Drake, Noah, 90
Driscoll, Ricky, 51, 55
Dru, Mitchell, 15
Dubeck, Frank, 75
DuBujaek, Max, 149
Dumonde, Renee, 63
Dunlap, Jason, 11
Duval, Martine, 122

Edwards, Tom, 11
Egan, Chris, 83
Eldredge, John, 11

INDEX

Eliot, Brad, 170
Eliot, Jane, 98
Eliot, Leslie, 170, 172, 174
Elliott, Stephen, 98
Ellison, Mary, 38
Emerson, Brian, 163
Emerson, Kristin, 163
Emerson, Preacher, 83
Enright, Mona, 105
Evans, Marlena, 62
Evans, Samantha, 56, 62
Ewing, Baby Jean, 20
Ewing, Blaine, 16, 20, 123
Ewing, Catlin, 20
Ewing, Clarice, 20
Ewing, Cory, 20, 21
Ewing, Larry, 20, 123

Fairchild III, Richard, 164
Fallon, Jessica, 67
Fallon, Joshua, 67
Faraday, Timmy, 76
Fargate, Myrtle, 5, 9
Fargo, Danny, 13
Fargo, Missy, 13
Farmer, Mitch, 11
Faulkner, Laura, 123
Fenelli, Jack, 141, 142, 143, 149
Fenelli, Mary, 142, 149
Fenelli, Ryan, 148
Fenmore, Neil, 176
Fenton, Gil, 18, 21
Ferguson, Edna, 5, 9
Ferguson, Martha, 152
Fickett, Mary, 152
Fleming, Fred, 90
Fleming, Janet, 90
Fletcher, Anne, 103
Fletcher, Jane, 105
Fletcher, John, 102, 103
Fletcher, Paul, 102, 103
Fletcher, Robin, 153
Flood, Ann, 74, 153
Forbes, Ann Alden, 120
Forbes, Jack, 116, 121
Forbes, Johnny, 115
Forbes, Lorna, 118
Forbes, Roger, 121
Ford, Constance, 153
Ford, Steven, 168
Forenza, Carlo, 67
Forsythe, Henderson, 10, 34

Foster, Greg, 123
Foster, Snapper, 169, 170
Foster, Tucker, 42
Frame, Alice, 16, 21
Frame, Jamie, 16, 21, 123
Frame, Sally, 16, 21, 139
Frame, Steve, 10, 14, 15
Francis, Genie, 123
Frank, Gary, 45
Franklyn, Shelley, 82
Froman, David, 122
Frye, Edith Hughes, 152
Fuller, Sara, 56

Gabriel, John, 10
Gallant, Felicia, 17, 21
Gallison, Joseph, 10
Galloway, Mark, 11
Gantz, Matthew, 82
Gardner, Bud, 158
Gardner, Janet, 158
Gardner, Jenny, 3
Gardner, Opal, 8
Gardner, Ray, 4, 8
Garretson, Rafe, 133
Garrison, Eric, 177
Garrison, Iris Donnelly, 153
Gentry, Robert, 10, 98
George, Christopher, 139
Gergman, Stu, 44
Gifford, Alan, 138
Glass, Katherine, 97
Gleason, Regina, 72
Goddard, Louise, 16
Goddard, Mark, 122
Gordon, Beatrice, 16
Gorrow, Vivien, 18, 20
Gracie, Sally, 97, 152
Graham, John, 98
Graham, Kenny, 148
Granger, Shelly, 48
Grant, Danny, 67
Grant, Dick, 101, 102
Grant, Marie, 103
Grant, Nancy, 2
Gray, Carla, 123
Gray, David, 56
Gray, Sadie, 133
Greenberg, Dave, 149
Greenberg, Rico, 149
Grey, Gordon, 90
Griffin, Lloyd, 11

Grimsley, Winston, 76
Groome, Malcolm, 145
Grubbs, Verla, 8

Hagman, Larry, 73
Haines, Larry, 157
Hale, Peg, 153
Hall, Ed, 126, 133
Hall, Sam, 129
Hamill, Mark, 45, 73
Hamilton, Brooke, 62, 63
Hamilton, David, 90
Hammond, Dane, 10, 121, 164
Hansen, Peter, 86
Harding, Quinn, 21
Harding, Thomasina, 21
Hardy, Audrey, 95
Hardy, Steve, 87, 95
Hardy, Tommy, 95
Harmon, Jennifer, 98
Harper, Kelly, 48, 49, 55
Harper, Mary, 75
Harper, Roger, 75
Harper, Scotty, 55
Harrington, Delphi, 97
Hart, Dick, 11
Haskell, Joe, 11
Haskins, Walter, 11
Hastings, Don, 10, 30
Hathaway, Julian, 11
Hathaway, Max, 66
Hathaway, Megan, 66
Hayes, Bill, 58
Hayes, George, 102
Hayes, Susan Seaforth, 58
Hays, Kathryn, 139
Henderson, Bruce, 171
Henderson, Mark, 171
Henderson, Quentin, 75
Herrera, Anthony, 10
Hewitt, Jeremy, 88
Hickland, 51
Hill, Tiffany, 95
Hillyer, Laura, 56
Hindman, Art, 117
Hobart, Jim, 89
Hobson, Ada, 20, 153
Hobson, Charlie, 18
Hodges, Melinda, 121
Hodges, Warren, 121
Hogan, Jonathan, 97
Holbrook, Hal, 73, 97

Holden, Mark, 101, 102
Holmes, Anne, 153
Holmes, Teddy, 11
Holt, Jimmy Lee, 95
Hopkins, Ina, 152
Horton, Addie, 59, 67
Horton, Alice, 62, 66, 72
Horton, Bill, 59, 60, 66
Horton, Bobby, 72
Horton, Danny, 72
Horton, Jennifer Rose, 63, 66
Horton, Kitty, 66, 72
Horton, Laura, 60, 67
Horton, Maggie, 67
Horton, Marie, 59, 60
Horton, Michael, 63, 67
Horton, Mickey, 59, 60, 66, 67
Horton, Sandy, 66, 72
Horton, Sarah, 67
Horton, Tom, 61, 67, 72
Horton, Tommy, 59, 60, 66, 72
Houghton, James, 123
Hoye, Gloria, 97, 98
Hubbard, Ace, 11
Hubbard, Angie, 8
Hubbard, Frank, 8
Hubbard, Jesse, 8
Huddleston, Talbot, 127
Hudson, Gary, 35
Hughes, Bob, 10, 30, 43
Hughes, Chris, 31, 43
Hughes, Frannie, 43
Hughes, Jennifer, 43, 153
Hughes, Margo, 38, 43
Hughes, Nancy, 31, 43
Hughes, Natalie, 38
Hughes, Pa, 31, 37
Hughes, Penny, 32
Hughes, Tom, 36, 37, 43
Hunter, Diane, 59
Hunter, Kim, 44
Hunter, Richard, 59
Hutchins, Carl, 18, 21
Hutchins, Perry, 20
Hutchinson, William, 128
Hyde, Bill, 148

Jackson, Jazz, 176
Jackson, Kate, 73
Jackson, Leslie, 102, 105
Jackson, Steve, 103, 105
Jamison, Kevin, 11

INDEX

Jannings, Pete, 66
Jannings, Tess, 66
Jean, Lettie, 5
Jefferson, Tara, 8
Jeffreys, Anne, 45
Jenkins, Diane, 174
Johnson, Caroline, 16
Jones, Anthony, 95
Jones, Christine, 98, 122
Jones, Frisco, 95
Jones, James Earl, 73
Jones, Roscoe, 52
Jones, Tommy Lee, 73

Kane, Eric, 2
Kane, Erica, 1, 26
Karackas, Andrea, 38
Karr, Laurie Ann, 80
Karr, Mary Vernon, 133
Karr, Mike, 75, 76, 77, 78, 83
Karr, Nancy, 74, 75, 76, 78, 83, 85, 122, 153
Karr, Sara, 56
Karras, Christina, 153
Keane, Teri, 44, 153
Keith, Susan, 152
Keller, Mary Page, 139
Kelly, Joe, 91
Kelly, Rose, 91, 94
Kemmer, Edward, 97
Kendall, Brian, 56
Kendall, Lloyd, 163
Kennicott, Betsy, 4
Kibbee, Lois, 79
Kincaid, Dan, 11
Kincaid, Hillary, 103
Kincaid, Simone, 103
Kingsley, Brandon, 3, 123
Kipling, Alan, 164
Kipling, Ivan, 127, 159
Kirkland, Amanda, 123
Kirkland, Hollis, 146
Knight, Ted, 97
Kositchek, Chris, 66
Kosloff, Sylvie, 16
Kramer, Harry, 80
Kramer, Mandel, 44

Lacrosse, Paul, 105
Lacy, Jerry, 98
Lahti, Gary, 35
Laire, Judson, 96, 97
Lake, Cindy, 172

Lammers, Paul, 97
Lamont, Felicia, 123
Landers, Audrey, 44
Lane, Jack, 11
Lang, Bob, 102
Langley, Spencer, 160
Lansing, Gary, 90
Larkin, John, 78
Lars, Steven, 90, 95
Lawrence, Elizabeth, 152
Lawson, Lee, 152
LeBlanc, Christian J., 39
LeClair, Dougie, 63
LeClair, Robert, 63
Lee, Anne, 153
Lemay, Harding, 15
Lester, Edy, 120
Lewis, Amy, 176
Lewis, Billy, 108
Lewis, Edwina, 132
Lewis, Frank, 176
Lewis, H. B., 109
Lewis, Josh, 109
Lewis, Mindy, 110
Lewis, Reva, 109, 152
Lewis, Trish, 108
Lewis, Vanessa, 26, 109
Lincoln, Rusty, 61
Lipton, John, 72
Locke, Ralph, 99
Lord, Victor, 126, 127
Lord, Victoria, 153
Lorimer, Eddie, 80
Love, Donna, 21, 26
Love, Marley, 21
Love, Nicole, 21
Love, Peter, 21
Lovell, Katherine, 152
Lowell, Jim, 32
Lowell, Judge, 32, 34
Lucas, Sam, 16
Lutz, Charles, 88, 90
Lutz, Emma, 90
Lyons, Philip, 11

MacDonnell, Ray, 3
Makana, Anthony, 10, 133
Mallory, Derek, 76, 83
Malone, Tracy, 153
Mandan, Robert, 98
Manzini, Helena, 105, 139
Marcantel, Chris, 10

THE SOAP OPERA *Digest* SCRAPBOOK

Marceau, Bill, 75, 76
Marceau, Martha, 75, 152
March, Lori, 99
March, Lucille, 88
Mars, Leo, 20
Marsh, Abel, 20
Marino, Jumbo, 143
Marler, Jackie, 104
Marler, Ross, 105, 108
Marshall, Alex, 60, 164
Marshall, Renee, 66
Martin, Ann, 9
Martin, Bobby, 3
Martin, David, 61, 63
Martin, Dick, 36
Martin, Dottie, 9
Martin, Doug, 157, 158, 162
Martin, Eunice, 157
Martin, Helen, 59
Martin, Jeff, 4, 8, 123
Martin, Joe, 1, 2, 3, 4, 8
Martin, Joey, Jr., 8
Martin, John, 59
Martin, Kate, 2, 8, 153
Martin, Mary, 4
Martin, Mitzie, 77, 83
Martin, Paul, 1, 8
Martin, Ruth, 1, 4, 8, 152
Martin, Stephanie, 56
Martin, Susan, 59
Martin, Tad, 4, 8
Martin, Tara, 123
Mason, Lily, 20
Masters, Marie, 138
Matthews, Alice, 152
Matthews, Bill, 11, 14
Matthews, Jim, 14, 18
Matthews, Liz, 12, 14, 17, 20, 26, 122
Matthews, Mary, 56
Matthews, Pat, 13
Matthews, Rachel, 14
Matthews, Russ, 14, 123
Matthews, Tracy, 56
Maxwell, Jason, 123
McCandless, Baxter, 47, 54
McCandless, Clarissa, 46, 47, 54
McCandless, Gillian, 3
McCandless, Julie, 51, 55
McCandless, Matt, 51, 54
McCandless, Thomas, 48, 49, 54
McCandless, Tyler, 54
McCandless, Wally, 48, 49, 54
McCarthy, Laura, 163

McColl, Brian, 42
McColl, Charmane, 42
McColl, Kirk, 39, 42
McColl, Lisa, 26, 42
McColl, Whit, 38, 42
McCord, Quinton, 105, 139
McDermot, Maxie, 133
McFadden, Bonnie, 8
McFadden, Devon, 4, 49
McFadden, Wally, 3, 8
McFarland, Ian, 11
McFarren, Ben, 103
McFarren, Eve, 139
McGowan, Gil, 18
McGowan, Nancy, 21
McGuire, Maeve, 138, 139
McGuire, Sally, 170
McIntyre, Marilyn, 117, 152
McIntyre, Sara, 103, 104
McKinnon, M. J., 20
McLeary, Adair, 162
McLeary, Cagney, 162
McLeary, Hogan, 162
McLeary, Kate, 162
McLeod, Augusta, 88
Meecham, Wade, 77
Melina, Rose, 143
Mercantel, Christopher, 114
Mercer, Greg, 44
Mercer, Peggy, 88
Metcalf, Fred, 156
Meyer, Jake, 94
Miller, Alma, 34
Milli, Robert, 122
Mills, Donna, 73
Mitchell, James, 10, 97
Mitchell, Ralph, 38
Moltke, Alexandra, 96
Montgomery, Craig, 42, 164
Montgomery, Danielle, 42
Montgomery, Lyla, 43
Moore, Helen, 16
Moore, Lenore, 14
Morgan, Mary Sue, 20
Morgan, R. J., 20
Morris, Amy, 44
Morris, Eve, 152
Morrison, Link, 11
Movotny, Tiso, 143
Murdock, Myra, 9, 152

Nelson, Enid, 8
Nelson, Gregg, 8

INDEX

Nelson, Jenny, 8
Nelson, Peggy, 90
Nettleton, Lois, 97
Newman, Julia, 173, 177
Newman, Nikki, 177
Newman, Victor, 173, 174, 177
Nichols, Josephine, 98
Nixon, Agnes, 6
Nolan, Peggy, 14
Noone, Kathleen, 6
Norris, Holly, 102
Norris, Stanley, 102, 103, 104
North, Heather, 72
North, Rebecca, 61, 63
Norton, Leonie, 44
Novak, Jacqueline, 149
Novak, Joe, 149
Novotny, Laslo, 148

Oehler, Gretchen, 18
Olson, Addie, 60
Olson, Ben, 59, 67
Olson, Julie, 59
Olson, Steve, 67
O'Neill, Connie, 133
O'Neill, Didi, 133
O'Neill, Harry, 132
O'Neill, Joy, 132
O'Reardon, Dennis, 128
Ousley, Jim, 2

Pace, Jennifer, 158
Page, Geraldine, 44
Palzis, Kelly, 3
Parker, Jameson, 73
Parrish, Blackie, 95
Parrish, Gwen, 16
Parrish, Leueen, 17
Patterson, Linda, 60, 63
Paulson, Ira, 11
Pavel, Michael, 144
Peabody, Rose, 152
Perelli, Lorna, 120
Perelli, Tony, 120
Perrini, Angie, 123
Perrini, Joey, 123
Perrini, Rose, 17
Peters, Audrey, 98
Peters, Eric, 61
Peters, Greg, 60
Peters, Phil, 61
Peters, Susan, 60
Phillips, Bryan, 89, 95

Phillips, Christine, 157
Phillips, Claudia, 95
Phillips, Ira, 129
Phillips, John, 157
Phillips, Kathy, 162
Phillips, Scott, 11, 157, 158, 162
Pickles, Christina, 138
Pinkham, Henry, 88
Pollock, Joe, 77
Pollock, Rose, 153
Pope, Tom, 32
Porter, Luke, 37, 38
Porter, Ralph, 37
Prentice, John, 89
Prentiss, Johnny, 139
Prentiss, Lauralee, 174
Price, Sydney, 148
Prince, William, 98
Prudence, 148
Putnam, Grant, 94

Quartermaine, Alan, 94
Quartermaine, Alan, Jr., 94
Quartermaine, Alexandria, 56
Quartermaine, Beatrice, 94
Quartermaine, Edward, 94
Quartermaine, Jason, 94
Quartermaine, Lila, 94
Quartermaine, Monica, 26, 94, 152

Raines, Beth, 108
Raines, Bradley, 108, 164
Raines, Lillian, 153
Ralston, Yancy, 128
Ramsey, Burt, 95
Ramsey, Claire, 108
Randall, Trip, 139
Randolph, John, 13
Randolph, Lee, 14
Randolph, Marianne, 16, 123
Randolph, Michael, 16
Rawlins, Janice, 4
Reade, Fletcher, 108
Reardon, Annabelle, 109
Reardon, Bea, 105, 109, 152
Reardon, Jim, 109
Reardon, Stacey, 109
Reardon, Tom, 109
Reardon, Tony, 109
Reed, Nikki, 139, 172, 174
Reeve, Christopher, 44, 73
Reid, Bob, 149
Reid, Delia, 142

THE **SOAP OPERA** *Digest* SCRAPBOOK

Reid, Frances, 72
Reinholdt, George, 15
Renaldi, David Reynolds, 10, 11, 132, 167
Renaldi, Jenny, 132
Reynolds, Andrea, 156, 157
Reynolds, Ann, 152
Reynolds, Brock, 123, 172
Reynolds, Jamie, 156, 157
Reynolds, Len, 156
Reynolds, Sam, 156, 157, 162
Richard, Andy, 174, 177
Richards, Diane, 177
Richards, Jennifer, 105
Riley, Joe, 122, 127, 132
Riley, Kevin, 132
Riley, Meagan, 122
Robbins, Carol, 177
Roberts, Joe, 101
Robinson, Bernice, 15
Rochelle, Dirk, 115
Rolland, Pierre, 170
Roma, Gina, 174, 176
Romalotti, Danny, 176
Rooney, Dan, 88, 94
Roskov, Boris, 95
Roskov, Tania, 94
Rowland, Jada, 97
Roy, Mike, 9
Roylance, Pamela, 72
Russell, Leo, 95
Ryan, Barry, 142
Ryan, Chuck, 36
Ryan, E. J., 144
Ryan, Frank, 142, 145, 149
Ryan, Johnny, 10, 142, 143, 149
Ryan, Little John, 149
Ryan, Maeve, 142, 148
Ryan, Pat, 145, 146, 148
Ryan, Rick, 35, 36
Ryan, Sean, 105
Ryan, Siobhan, 143, 148
Ryan, Tim, 122

Sago, Estelle, 5
St. George, Louis, 17, 159
Sanders, Carrie, 3
Sarandon, Susan, 73
Sawyer, Anna, 59
Sawyer, Carl, 59
Saxon, Deborah, 77
Saxon, Geraldine, 76, 79, 80, 82
Saxon, Tony, 75, 77

Schenk, Lucinda, 133
Scorpio, Holly, 94
Scorpio, Robert, 94
Scott, April, 84
Scott, Ben, 102
Scott, Carla, 133
Scott, Draper, 84
Scott, Jack, 126
Scott, Maggie, 103
Scott, Michael, 173
Scott, Peggy, 103
Selleck, Tom, 73
Sentell, Elan, 162
Sentell, Liza, 162
Sentell, Mignon, 163
Sentell, Rusty, 163
Sentell, T. R., 163
Sentell, Tourneur, 163
Sentell, Travis, 160, 163
Shaffer, Lorena, 94
Shaffer, Louise, 97
Shea, Harry, 138
Shea, Michael, 35, 36
Shea, Pete, 11
Shearer, Julia, 21
Shearer, Susan, 16
Shelby, Ben, 149
Shelby, Bess, 149
Shelby, Maggie, 149
Shepherd, Adrian, 4
Sherwood, Lynn, 152
Shoberg, Richard, 10
Simmons, Allison, 156
Simon, Peter, 10
Singleton, Mark, 21
Skelly, Bert, 126
Slater, Garth, 56, 117, 164
Slater, Lily, 114, 115, 117, 118
Slezak, Erica, 122, 124
Sloan, Tina, 153
Sloane, Shana, 117, 120, 152
Smith, Sally, 152
Smith, Viola, 153
Sparer, Paul, 98
Spaulding, Alan, 104, 105, 164
Spaulding, Brandon, 56, 105
Spaulding, Elizabeth, 104, 105
Spaulding, Jackie, 104, 105
Spaulding, Mindy Lewis, 108
Spaulding, Phillip, 105, 108
Spencer, Bobbie, 26, 88
Spencer, Gillian, 153

INDEX

Spencer, Laura, 94, 123
Spencer, Luke, 94, 123
Spode, Martin, 11
Stafford, Jane Marie, 105
Stafford, Janice, 105
Stallings, Amy, 38
Stallings, Carol, 38
Stallings, Jay, 38
Steele, Matt, 11, 98
Stenbeck, Barbara, 36, 43
Stenbeck, Gunnar, 37, 43
Stenbeck, James, 11, 37, 43, 164
Stenbeck, Paul, 43
Sterling, Bruce, 45
Stevens, April, 173
Stevens, Ken, 11
Stevens, Paul, 10
Stewart, Annie, 123
Stewart, Betty, 33
Stewart, Dan, 33, 37, 42
Stewart, David, 10, 33, 34, 35, 42
Stewart, Dee, 123
Stewart, Don, 110
Stewart, Elizabeth, 56
Stewart, Ellen, 32, 36, 42
Stone, Zachary, 43
Stoner, Calvin, 76, 83
Stoner, Didi, 82
Stoner, Quincy, 15
Sterling, Barbara, 153
Sterling, Bruce, 44
Strasser, Robin, 152
Stuart, Mary, 154
Sullivan, Tim, 177
Swift, Jamey, 83
Swift, Logan, 82

Tate, Arthur, 156
Tate, Sue, 156
Taylor, Diana, 122
Taylor, Peter, 89
Tesreau, Krista, 110
Thatcher, Kevin, 21
Thinnes, Roy, 45
Thomas, Richard, 139
Thompson, Art, 145
Thompson, Cathleen, 145
Thompson, Katie, 148
Thompson, Marcy, 42
Thorne, Sybil, 4, 138
Thornton, David, 2
Thornton, Dottie, 3, 6

Thorpe, Adam, 102
Thorpe, Barbara Norris, 45, 104
Thorpe, Liz, 152
Thorpe, Roger, 11, 56, 104, 164, 167
Thurston, Arnold, 88
Thurston, Derek, 173
Tippit, Wayne, 97
Tomm, Ron, 96
Tourneur, Gen. Roger, 164
Tourneur, Joanne, 154, 155, 163
Tourneur, Martin, 164
Towers, Constance, 46
Trainer, Price, 126
Travis, Jody, 78, 83, 85
Travis, Larry, 35
Travis, Nicole, 78
Tuggle, Billy Clyde, 4
Turino, Joe, 103
Turner, Ron, 117
Twining, Rex, 156
Tyler, Amy, 8
Tyler, Charles, 2, 9
Tyler, Chuck, 9
Tyler, Damien, 80
Tyler, Donna, 5
Tyler, Judson, 47, 54
Tyler, Kelly, 8
Tyler, Kitty, 56
Tyler, Lincoln, 1, 9
Tyler, Mona, 2, 9
Tyler, Phoebe, 1, 2
Tyson, Cicely, 73

Valenza, Tasia, 6
Van Dine, Alicia, 77, 82
Van Patten, Dick, 73
Vanderpoole, Alfred, 8
Vane, Lahoma, 14
Vartova, Alexei, 144
Vernon, Brad, 133
Vernon, Naomi, 152
Vernon, Samantha, 133, 153
Vernon, Will, 44, 126, 133
Vested, David, 104
Vested, Kit, 104
Vincente, Jo, 158, 159
Vincente, Tony, 56, 158
Vincente, Wendy, 158, 160
Vining, Amy, 95
Vining, Barbara, 90
Vochek, Jim, 115, 117, 121
Vochek, Merrill, 115, 116, 121

213

Vochek, Noreen, 115
Voightlander, Kurt, 48, 49, 50
Von Halkein, Alexandra, 108

Wade, Neil, 34
Wagner, Gunther, 79, 82, 122
Wagner, Marge, 152
Wainwright, Phillip, 123
Wallace, Robert, 11
Walling, Brad, 11
Wallingford, Langley, 9
Wallingford, Phoebe, x, 9, 26, 152
Walter, Jessica, 73
Walton, Dan, 158, 162
Walton, Gary, 158, 162
Ward, Annie, 42
Ward, Jeff, 42
Ward, Lowell, 42
Ward, Maria, 42
Ward, Nancy, 42
Warfield, Simon, 132
Warner, Bobby, 9, 138
Warner, Cliff, 4, 9
Warner, Linda, 9
Warner, Nina, 9
Warren, Lynn Wilkins, 153
Warrick, Ruth, x, 152
Watson, Douglass, 10, 12
Wayland, Len, 98
Webber, Helene, 95
Webber, Jeff, 91, 95
Webber, Lars, 90, 95
Webber, Lesley, 56, 95
Webber, Mike, 95
Webber, Rick, 89, 90, 91, 95
Weeks, Al, 89
Wells, Lindsay, 177
Werner, Joe, 11, 122
Werner, Tim, 11
West, Josh, 126
Westheimer, Marshall, 142
Westheimer, Ruth, 142
Wexler, Amanda, 105, 139
Wexler, Jennifer, 105
Wheeler, Carrie, 44
Whipple, Alice, 153
White, Ted, 101, 102
Whiting, Andrea, 162
Whiting, Len, 162

Whiting, Patti, 153, 163
Whitman, Georgina, 138
Whitney, Colin, 11, 122
Whitney, Gordon, 80
Whitney, Keith, 138
Whitney, Raven, 26, 76, 77, 82
Whitney, Schuyler, 79, 82
Whittaker, Fran, 152
Wiggins, Tudi, 98
Wilkins, Stephanie, 158, 159, 160
Williams, Addie, 61, 63
Williams, Ann, 98
Williams, Carl, 173, 176
Williams, Doug, 58, 60, 62, 63, 67
Williams, Hope, 63, 67
Williams, Jobeth, 73
Williams, Julie, 58, 67
Williams, Lauren, 176
Williams, Mary, 173, 176
Williams, Mitch, 94
Williams, Paul, 168, 172, 176
Williams, Tracy, 94
Wilson, Chuck, 128, 132
Wilson, Hillary, 8
Wind, Far, 11
Winter, Edward, 138
Witherspoon, Walter, 127
Winthrop, Cass, 18, 21
Winthrop, Jeremy, 148
Winthrop, Stacey, 138
Wolek, Anna, 127
Wolek, Dan, 125, 127, 132
Wolek, Jenny, 138
Wolek, Karen, 127, 138
Wolek, Larry, 132
Wolek, Wanda, 132, 153
Woodard, Rae, 26, 45, 144
Woods, Robert S., 127
Wright, Courtney, 133
Wyatt, Eunice, 163
Wyatt, John, 158, 163
Wyatt, Stephanie, 26, 163
Wyatt, Suzi, 163
Wyndham, Victoria, 153

Yeager, Joanna, 9

Zaslow, Michael, 10, 167
Zimmer, Kim, 152